500

NEBRASKA WILDLIFE VIEWING GUIDE

Joseph Knue

D1384537

FALCON

Helena, Montana

Design, typesetting, and other prepress work by Falcon Press®, Helena, Montana.
Printed in Malaysia.

ISBN 1-56044-512-2

Front cover photo: Sandhill crane by Mike Forsberg.
Back cover photos: Regal fritillary butterfly by Mike Forsberg; mule deer by Bob Grier.

Library of Congress Cataloging-in-Publication Data
Knue, Joseph.
        Nebraska wildlife viewing guide / Joseph Knue.
            p.   cm.
        Includes index.
        ISBN 1-56044-512-2 (pbk.)
        1. Wildlife viewing sites—Nebraska—Guidebooks. 2.Wildlife
        watching—Nebraska—Guidebooks. 3. Nebraska—Guidebooks.
        I. Title.
        QL189.K58   1997
        599.09782—dc20   96-36463
                                                                           CIP

CONTENTS

PROJECT SPONSORS

The NEBRASKA GAME AND PARKS COMMISSION's mission is: Stewardship of the state's fish, wildlife, park, and outdoor recreation resources in the best long-term interests of the people and those resources. Nebraska Game and Parks Commission, 2200 N. 33rd Street, P.O. Box 30370, Lincoln, NE 68503; (402) 471-0641.

DEFENDERS OF WILDLIFE is a nonprofit organization of more than 100,000 members and supporters dedicated to preserving the natural abundance and diversity of wildlife and its habitat. A 1-year membership is $20 and includes a subscription to *Defenders,* an award-winning conservation magazine. To join, or for further information: Defenders of Wildlife, 1101 14th Street NW, Suite 1400, Washington, D.C. 20005; (202) 682-9400.

The USDA FOREST SERVICE is mandated by law to manage for multiple uses and sustained yields of renewable resources such as water, forage, wildlife, and recreation on National Forests and Grasslands. The Forest Service, in consultation with the public, determines the best combination of uses to benefit the American people and to assure continued land productivity and environmental quality. Our mission is "Caring for the land and serving the people." Nebraska National Forest, 125 North Main St., Chadron, NE 69337; (308) 432-0300.

In support of the BUREAU OF RECLAMATION's current mission to become the premier water management agency in the world, Reclamation strives to manage and protect water and related resources for both consumptive and non-consumptive uses in an environmentally sound manner. In light of its direct parallel with our goals, the Bureau of Reclamation enthusiastically supports the Watchable Wildlife program in Nebraska. Contact: Bureau of Reclamation, Nebraska-Kansas Area Office, Box 1607, Grand Island, NE 68802; (308) 389-4623.

The U.S. FISH AND WILDLIFE SERVICE is pleased to support this project in furtherance of its mission to conserve, protect, and enhance fish and wildlife resources and their habitats for the continuing benefit of the American public. Service programs include the national wildlife refuge system, protection of threatened and endangered species, conservation of migratory birds, fisheries restoration, outdoor recreation and education, wildlife research, and law enforcement. For more information contact: U.S. Fish and Wildlife Service, Region 6, P.O. Box 25486, Denver Federal Center, Denver, CO 80225; (303) 236-7905.

The NEBRASKA DEPARTMENT OF ROADS' mission is to provide and maintain, in cooperation with public and private organizations, a safe, effective, affordable, and coordinated statewide transportation system for the movement of people and goods. NDOR's vision: We are a skilled, respected, motivated, and diversified team. We will be recognized as the nation's leading transportation department, the most efficient, effective, and responsive state agency, and a model for other organizations. Nebraska Department of Roads, 1500 Nebraska Highway 2, P.O. Box 94759, Lincoln, NE 68509-4759; (402) 471-4567.

The NEBRASKA DIVISION OF TRAVEL AND TOURISM is pleased to play a role in sharing the abundant wildlife viewing opportunities presented in this book. For several years now surveys completed by the traveling public have indicated the enormous popularity of viewing wildlife in pristine and natural settings. We hope you enjoy your experiences in Nebraska and invite you to call 800-228-4307 for more tourism information about our great state.

THE CENTRAL NEBRASKA PUBLIC POWER AND IRRIGATION DISTRICT operates Nebraska's largest irrigation project which provides multiple benefits of surface water irrigation service to more than 112,000 acres, hydroelectric power, wildlife habitat, recreational opportunities, and ground water recharge. Central's mission is to serve the agricultural-based community in south-central Nebraska by protecting and utilizing available natural resources in a sustainable and ecologically balanced manner to provide reliable surface water irrigation, ground water recharge, electric power, and recreational opportunities while preserving and enhancing the quality of life and the natural environment in the region. Contact Central at 415 Lincoln St., P.O. Box 740, Holdrege, NE 68949-0740; (308) 995-8601.

DEPARTMENT OF DEFENSE (DOD) is the steward of about 25 million acres of land in the United States, many of which possess irreplaceable natural and cultural resources. The DOD is pleased to support the Watchable Wildlife Program through its Legacy Resource Management Program, a special initiative to enhance the conservation and restoration of natural and cultural resources on military land. For more information contact the Office of the Deputy Under Secretary of Defense (Environmental Security), 400 Navy Drive, Suite 206, Arlington, VA 22202-2884.

INTRODUCTION

Except for the border formed by the Missouri River, Nebraska's boundaries are entirely arbitrary. You will not find anything in the landscape to tell you where they are. They are not drawn around any natural feature or region. In fact, the boundaries of Nebraska circumscribe slices of much larger regions extending far to the north, south, east, and west.

Nebraska contains a slice of the tallgrass prairie region more typical east of the state. It contains some of the mixed-grass and shortgrass prairies of the Great Plains that extend north into Saskatchewan and south into Texas. It contains "fingers" of the ponderosa pine forest typical of the Black Hills and the Rocky Mountains—the forest's easternmost limit. Even the oak-hickory forest of the midwest reaches its western limit in Nebraska. The place we call "Nebraska" is, on the ground, a place where plant and wildlife communities reach their northern, southern, eastern, and western limits, giving Nebraska a rich biodiversity and, therefore, abundant wildlife viewing opportunities.

It's not enough to say that Nebraska has both prairies and rivers. The Platte and the Missouri, for example, are very different rivers. The Missouri explored by Lewis and Clark was a fast-flowing river, its floodplain heavily timbered, and its oxbows and side channels providing marshes and backwaters for multitudes of wildlife species. The Platte then had a wide, shallow, braided channel, with sandbars scoured clean of woody vegetation. Along much of its length, this provided safe roosting sites for migrating cranes and waterfowl and attractive nesting sites for least terns, piping plovers, and other mid-stream nesters. Both rivers are changed today, yet they remain very different environments.

Nebraska lies in the heart of the Great Plains, yet within its borders there is considerable landscape variety and plant and animal diversity. BOB GRIER

Nor are the prairies all alike. The prairie of the Sandhills is a different biome than the mixed-grass prairie to the south. It is so different that it is given its own name—sandhills prairie. In the Sandhills the vegetation is sparse, the sand often shows between plants, and the grasses (for example, sand bluestem, prairie sandreed, sand dropseed, little bluestem, needle and thread, and hairy grama) are adapted to the well-drained dunes. Mixed-grass prairies on heavier soils support western wheatgrass, side-oats grama, blue grama, and buffalo grass.

The plant and wildlife landscape of Nebraska is much changed since settlement. Rivers no longer flow and change course the way they used to; agriculture and grazing have altered the abundance and diversity of plants on the prairies. Yet much remains. This book is meant to help you explore the prairies, forests, and wetlands of Nebraska and view the wildlife that has adapted to them. As you visit these mostly out-of-the-way places, you will become part of the latest phase of Nebraska's tradition of wildlife appreciation and conservation. Walk lightly.

THE NATIONAL WATCHABLE WILDLIFE PROGRAM

The National Watchable Wildlife Program is a nationwide cooperative effort to combine wildlife conservation with America's growing interest in wildlife-related outdoor recreation. The concept of the program is simple: People want to watch wildlife, and they want to watch wildlife in natural settings. But they don't always know where to go; they don't know when to go; and they don't know what to expect when they get there. The National Watchable Wildlife Program is designed to answer those needs. Each participating state identifies its best places for viewing wildlife; a uniform system of road signs (the binoculars logo you see on the cover of this guide) is put in place to help direct travelers; and guidebooks like this one give wildlife enthusiasts specific information about the sites.

It takes a lot of cooperative effort to establish such a program. In Nebraska, the Watchable Wildlife Program is a partnership of state and federal agencies and private conservation groups, each providing not only technical help but essential funding to produce the guidebook and establish the network of road signs. As time goes on, sites will be enhanced with trails, viewing blinds and platforms, and interpretive material such as signs, bird and animal lists, and brochures.

The goal of the Watchable Wildlife Program is to make wildlife viewing fun. But in a larger context, the Watchable Wildlife Program is about conservation. It is founded on the notion that, given opportunities to enjoy and learn about wildlife in natural settings, people will become advocates for conservation in the future. **The success of wildlife conservation everywhere depends on the interest and active involvement of citizens.** Use this guide to make your wildlife watching trips fun and successful; use it to discover Nebraska in new ways; and as you travel around Nebraska, remember that these places can only exist with the support of interested citizens like you. Support conservation efforts in every way you can.

TIPS FOR VIEWING WILDLIFE

Wildlife watching is an uncertain business. You're never sure what you're going to see or even if you'll see anything at all. But there are things you can do to increase your chances of seeing wild animals in natural settings.

• **Be Prepared.** It's not as trivial as it sounds. Before you visit, review site descriptions and viewing information for services, road conditions, and so on. Use maps—the U.S. Forest Service, the Nebraska Game and Parks Commission, or other public agencies might have just the information you are looking for. Carry water, even in winter. And remember, Nebraska's weather can change abruptly. In summer that might mean rain and hail; in spring, wind-driven snow. Pay attention to the forecast and bring appropriate clothing.

• **Pick Your Season.** Some wildlife species are only active or present in certain seasons. For example, the best times for viewing waterfowl in Nebraska are during the spring and fall migrations, especially spring. Bald eagles are best viewed in winter and spring. Check the information in the guide or call site managers to get detailed information regarding seasonal opportunities.

• **Pick the Time of Day.** The single most important way to increase your chances of seeing wildlife is to be there at dawn. Dusk is also good. Trying to watch wildlife during the midday heat of summer is likely to be a disappointment.

• **Use Field Guides.** Even the most experienced wildlife watchers depend on field guides for positive identification of plants and animals. Many guidebooks also help by identifying preferred habitats and habits for different species.

• **Use Binoculars or a Spotting Scope.** Binoculars come in different sizes— 7x35, 8x40, and 10x50 are common sizes. The first number refers to the magnification—how many times larger an object will appear. The second number refers to the diameter of the objective lens. The larger the lens, the more light that can enter. A lot of wildlife viewing goes on in low-light situations, so the bigger the lens you can bear to lug around, the better you will be able to see.

• **Move Slowly and Quietly.** Try to blend into your surroundings, either by using a blind—your car works very well—or by wearing neutral-colored clothing and keeping still. If you walk, walk slowly, stopping often to look and listen. Use trees and other vegetation as blinds.

VIEWING ETHICS

• **Keep Your Distance.** This applies to any wildlife you may encounter, including roosting sites. Binoculars and scopes allow you to get a good view without getting too close. Approach wildlife slowly, quietly, and indirectly. Always leave animals an avenue for retreat. If your presence causes animals to change their behavior, you are too close.

• **Respect Nests.** This also goes for denning sites and rookeries. Well-meaning but intrusive visitors may cause parents to flee, leaving the young vulnerable to the elements or predators. Stay on designated trails.

• **Leave Young Animals Alone.** Young animals that appear alone usually have parents waiting nearby.

• **Leave Pets at Home.** They may chase, startle, or even kill wildlife.

• **Don't Feed the Animals.** Animals do best on their natural foods. Animals that get hooked on handouts may eventually lose their fear of cars, campers, or even poachers.

• **Respect the Rights of Private Landowners.** Many of the sites in this guide are adjacent to private lands. This is especially true of areas along the Platte River where sandhill cranes feed during migration. Pull as far off roadways as you can, and remain in your vehicle. Do not venture onto private property unless you have obtained permission from the landowner. Respect fences and gates.

• **Respect the Rights of Other Viewers.** Keep quiet. If other people are viewing, allow them to enjoy a quality experience too. Leave places in better condition than you found them—if you find litter, pick it up and dispose of it properly.

Binoculars are essential equipment for watching wildlife, allowing close-up viewing without disturbing the animals. BOB GRIER

HOW TO USE THIS GUIDE

This guide divides Nebraska into four regions. Although the divisions are along highway lines and county lines, the regions generally correspond to four "vegetation zones" in Nebraska. The **Eastern** region roughly corresponds to what once was the tallgrass prairie zone in Nebraska. The **South-Central** region was largely mixed-grass prairie, and contains the Big Bend area of the central Platte River and the Rainwater Basin. The **Sandhills** region is the large dunefield that makes up the north-central part of Nebraska. The **Panhandle** is a high plains zone of mixed-grass and shortgrass prairie with some interesting topographic features—the Pine Ridge, the Wildcat Hills, and the North Platte River Valley.

Each region begins with a map that shows the general location of each site in the region and identifies it by number. Each viewing site entry contains a **description** of the site—the general lay of the land, an overview of the kinds of habitats the site contains, and unique or representative wildlife at the site (not necessarily everything you may encounter). **Viewing information** rounds out the picture, with notes on the best seasons for viewing, particular opportunities to take advantage of, and, occasionally, precautions. These include road and trail conditions, safety, viewing limitations, and land-ownership limitations. *SUCH CAUTIONARY NOTES APPEAR IN CAPITAL LETTERS.*

Written **directions** are given for each site. These directions are based on highway maps and county maps. These descriptions are not meant to take the place of state maps and county atlases. Sites in Nebraska are not hard to find, but driving distances can be unexpectedly long, and much of the state, especially in the Sandhills, is sparsely populated.

Facilities and recreation icons appear at the bottom of each site entry. The icons, identified on page 15, provide important information about facilities, recreational opportunities, fees, parking, and restrooms.

Wildlife Management Areas and Waterfowl Production Areas: Hunting is allowed on almost all wildlife management areas and waterfowl production areas. Be sure to check for season opening dates and closing dates. Many WMAs have a spring turkey season. Primitive camping is allowed on all WMAs, but they rarely have developed camp facilities. Call the contact numbers listed for individual sites if you have questions.

ABBREVIATIONS

COE	U.S. Army Corps of Engineers	USBR	Bureau of Reclamation
NGPC	Nebraska Game & Parks Commission	USFS	USDA Forest Service
NPS	National Park Service	USFWS	U.S. Fish & Wildlife Service
NWR	National Wildlife Refuge	WMA	Wildlife Management Area
SRA	State Recreation Area	WPA	Waterfowl Production Area

THE SPRING MIGRATION

It happens every year, more predictable in Nebraska than spring weather. A few arrive in the middle of February, then more and more. Sandhill cranes. Canada geese, snow geese, white-fronted geese, and Ross's geese. Ducks—teal, mallards, pintails, wigeons, and shovelers. Vast numbers of birds—half a million sandhill cranes, eight to ten million ducks and geese—fill an 80-mile stretch of the central Platte River and a region of scattered wetlands to the south called the Rainwater Basin.

Nowhere else in the world can you see such spectacles. For a short span of weeks, Nebraska plays host to 80 percent of the world's lesser sandhill cranes, 90 percent of the midcontinent population of greater white-fronted geese, more than a million snow geese, and hundreds of thousands of shorebirds. For most of these species, the migration route from southern wintering grounds to northern breeding sites narrows like an hourglass over Nebraska. These birds spend a few weeks, from late February through April, feeding and resting, preparing for the flight and the coming breeding season.

The *Nebraska Wildlife Viewing Guide* features many sites to view this migration spectacle. Harvard Waterfowl Production Area, for example, may host as many as 500,000 ducks and geese. From blinds at the Lillian Annette Rowe Sanctuary or Mormon Island Crane Meadows, you can look out over the river and wet meadows where 60,000 cranes may roost and feed. An estimated 80,000 people visit here each spring to watch and celebrate the migration at events such as "Wings Over the Platte" in Grand Island, or the "Spring Wing Ding" in Clay

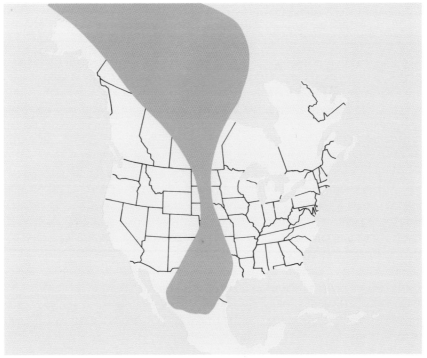

For many birds, the migration route from southern wintering grounds to northern breeding sites narrows like an hourglass over Nebraska.

Rainwater basins in Nebraska's intensively farmed south-central region provide critical habitat for migrating ducks and geese. JON FARRAR

Center. The cranes and waterfowl have been using this region for thousands of years, longer than any use by man. This region is considered critical to the birds as a migration stopover and as a key to a successful breeding season. But management of this area is a source of controversy in Nebraska.

Cranes and the Central Platte

The Platte River in Nebraska was once a true prairie river—sandy-bottomed, wide-channelled, and shallow. Spring floods swept its banks and sandbars clear of woody vegetation; wet meadows and marshes covered much of the floodplain. It was, in short, ideal habitat for sandhill cranes, which roost in shallow waters and feed in wet meadows. Once, migrating cranes used many miles of the Platte River. Today, however, demands for flood control and irrigation water have reduced flows in the Platte by 70 percent, and woody vegetation has encroached on the channel and sandbars. Crane habitat along the Platte today lies primarily in two sections totaling about 80 miles. Most biologists think the habitat in this remaining area is critical to the birds (there is no other place left for them to go) and that maintaining a certain level of water in the river is critical to the habitat. But the demand for water is always increasing, and we may yet test the biologists' theories in a real-life laboratory. If the biologists are wrong, the birds will survive. But there will be no satisfaction for the biologists in being right.

Geese, Ducks, and the Rainwater Basin

The Rainwater Basin is an area of flat to gently rolling plains formed over thousands of years by deep deposits of wind-blown silt or "loess." In wind-excavated depressions (basins) throughout the region, rainwater and snowmelt have leached and concentrated clay particles in the subsoils. When wet, the soil in these basins becomes plastic and nearly impervious to water. The basins trap runoff water, creating natural marshes. Once there were nearly 4,000 major wetlands in the Rainwater Basin, totaling nearly 100,000 acres. Today, perhaps

Piping plovers are sometimes mistaken for the more common killdeer. Plovers can be recognized by their single black breast band. JON FARRAR

only 10 percent of the original wetlands remain. Thus the wetlands that remain provide critical stopovers to millions of migrating birds.

Loss of wetlands is a problem across the continent, so much so that a continent-wide plan—the North American Waterfowl Management Plan—has been adopted by the United States, Canada, and Mexico to protect waterfowl habitat. The Rainwater Basin has been identified as a critical part of that plan. The Rainwater Basin Joint Venture has been established as a cooperative effort among landowners, private interests, and government agencies to protect, restore, enhance, and manage wetland resources in the Rainwater Basin.

More than a million snow geese migrate through Nebraska. The best viewing time is in the fall, usually in late November.
KEN BOUC

NEBRASKA

Wildlife Viewing Sites

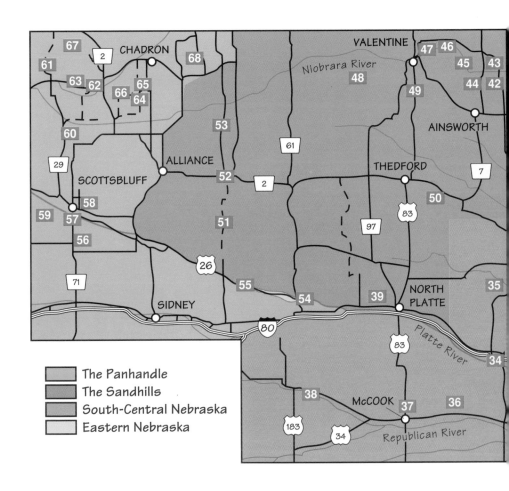

The Panhandle
The Sandhills
South-Central Nebraska
Eastern Nebraska

HIGHWAY SIGNS
As you travel in Nebraska and other states, look for these signs on interstates, highways, and other roads. They identify the route to follow to reach wildlife viewing sites.

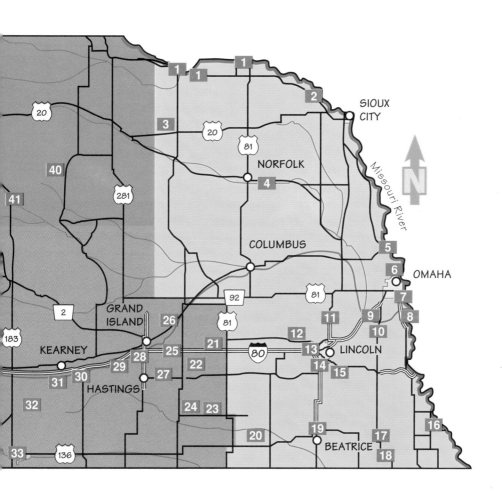

FACILITIES AND RECREATION

Parking   Entry Fee or Use Fee   Restrooms   Barrier Free   Picnic   Cross-country Skiing   Horse Trails

Camping   Hiking   Bicycling   Boat Ramp   Large Boats   Small Boats

REGION 1: EASTERN NEBRASKA

The eastern third of Nebraska was once tallgrass prairie—a sea of grasses that could grow waist high or even head high. Tallgrass prairie, with its mix of tall-growing grasses, wildflowers, and other plants, grew in the part of Nebraska where annual rainfall averages 25 inches or more. Reliable annual rainfall and rich soil made this prime agricultural land, and today most of the tallgrass prairie has been plowed. Remaining tracts of tallgrass prairie are small and scattered, and only a few have a good diversity of grasses and wildflowers. Sites such as Nine-Mile Prairie (Site 13) near Lincoln and Burchard Lake (Site 17) in southeastern Nebraska are examples. At other sites—Homestead National Monument of America (Site 19), for example—efforts are being made to "restore" the prairie to native species and to its former diversity, a long-term process that, because of the complexity of the system, may never be entirely successful.

Both the lower Platte River and the Missouri River flow through the eastern region of Nebraska. Here the Platte, in contrast with the central Platte, maintains its nature as a true prairie river. High spring flows, fed by the Elkhorn and Loup rivers, still scour sandbars free of woody vegetation and maintain a wide channel. Adjacent wet meadows and wetlands are relatively abundant. The lower Platte provides essential habitat for least terns and piping plovers. Platte River State Park (Site 10) provides vistas of the lower Platte from high observation towers.

The Missouri River forms the eastern border of Nebraska. The bluff forest along the Missouri River corridor is eastern deciduous forest, dominated by bur oak, black oak, basswood, green ash, and hackberry. This forest is home to wildlife species that are unusual in the state. Gray squirrels, southern flying squirrels, woodchucks, and timber rattlesnakes live only in deciduous forest sites in southeastern Nebraska, sites such as Indian Cave State Park (Site 16) or Fontenelle Forest (Site 7).

The floodplain forest along the Missouri is much changed from presettlement times, largely because of changes to the river. The Missouri has been dammed and channeled for flood control and barge traffic. As a result, the great spring and early summer floods no longer form new sandbars and seedbeds for cottonwoods and willows. Control of the river has allowed the floodplain forest to be converted to cropland. Consequently, it is now of less value to wildlife.

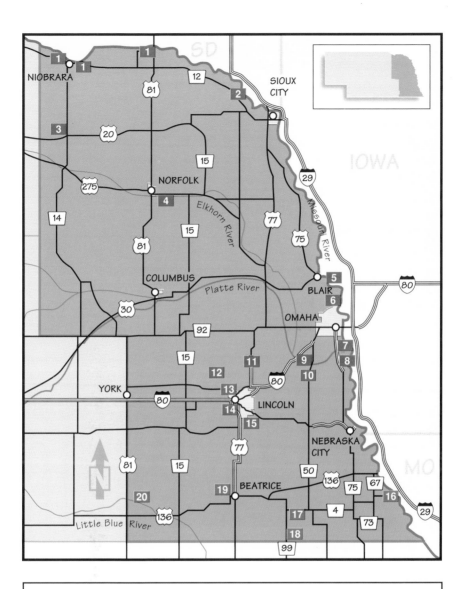

Wildlife Viewing Sites

1. Niobrara State Park, Bazile Creek Wildlife Management Area, Gavins Point Dam
2. Ponca State Park
3. Grove Lake Wildlife Management Area
4. Wood Duck Wildlife Management Area
5. DeSoto National Wildlife Refuge
6. Neale Woods Nature Center
7. Fontenelle Forest Nature Center
8. Randall W. Schilling Wildlife Area
9. Schramm Park State Recreation Area and Ak-Sar-Ben Aquarium Outdoor Education Center
10. Platte River State Park
11. Jack Sinn Memorial Wildlife Management Area
12. Branched Oak Wildlife Management Area
13. Nine-Mile Prairie
14. Pioneers Park Nature Center
15. Wilderness Park
16. Indian Cave State Park
17. Burchard Lake Wildlife Management Area
18. Pawnee Prairie Wildlife Management Area
19. Homestead National Monument of America
20. Meridian Wildlife Management Area

1. NIOBRARA STATE PARK, BAZILE CREEK WILDLIFE MANAGEMENT AREA, GAVINS POINT DAM

Description: Three tracts of public land that offer a broad spectrum of habitats and viewing opportunities. Niobrara State Park overlooks the confluence of the Niobrara and Missouri rivers. Just downstream, Bazile Creek WMA contains river woodlands, backwaters, and marshes. Twenty-five miles farther, Gavins Point Dam, the lowest of the main-stem dams on the Missouri River, forms Lewis and Clark Lake. As the Niobrara empties its sand load into the sediment-poor Missouri, a large delta is being formed at the upper end of Lewis and Clark Lake, attracting wading birds and waterfowl.

Viewing Information: One of the best viewing opportunities at Niobrara State Park is a 2.1-mile-long wheelchair-accessible trail over the entire northern boundary of the park, including the rivers' confluence. The trail traverses the river and marsh habitats of the park, with good viewing of water birds and other animals that use the river for habitat and water. Bazile Creek WMA offers excellent spring, summer, and fall opportunities to view wading birds such as great blue herons, green herons, and great egrets as well as an occasional chance to view muskrats and beavers. Wintering bald eagles, waterfowl, and gulls can be viewed October through March from the visitor center at Gavins Point Dam. Freshwater fish can be viewed at the Gavins Point Aquarium. There is a nature trail in the Gavins Point section of the Lewis and Clark Recreation Area. Bazile Creek is likely to be wet; rubber boots or waders are recommended for walking in the WMA.

Directions: *The entrance to NIOBRARA STATE PARK is approximately 2 miles west of the town of Niobrara on Nebraska Highway 12; BAZILE CREEK WMA lies along the north side of NE 12 from the east edge of Niobrara to the Bazile Creek Bridge (approximately 5 miles). Continue on NE 12 to Crofton, then go north on NE 121 approximately 9 miles to GAVINS POINT DAM.*

Ownership: Niobrara State Park and Bazile Creek WMA: NGPC (402) 857-3373 or (402) 857-3374; Gavins Point Dam: COE (402) 667-7873

Size: Niobrara State Park: 1,200 acres; Bazile Creek WMA: 4,500 acres

Closest towns: Niobrara and Crofton

American avocets are usually seen wading in shallow water, stirring up food from the muddy bottom by moving their long turned-up bill from side to side. Their feet are webbed like a duck's feet, and they can swim well.

2. PONCA STATE PARK

Description: A popular park for winter and summer recreation, Ponca State Park overlooks one of the few unchanneled stretches of the Missouri River. Habitats are predominantly bur oak, basswood, green ash, and hackberry forest. Popular viewing species include white-tailed deer, fox squirrels, and raccoons. The Missouri is a migration corridor for songbirds and waterfowl, so during spring and fall look for songbirds, snow geese, and ducks. In winter look for bald eagles overhead. In summer look for turkey vultures. Spring wildflowers include dutchman's breeches, bloodroot, and dogtooth violet.

Viewing Information: The best opportunities for viewing come from more than 17 miles of hiking trails. Trail maps and brochures are available from the park office. Some of these trails are available for horseback riding and for cross-country skiing.

Directions: From the junction of Nebraska Highway 12 and Spur 26E in Ponca, take Spur 26E 2 miles north to the park entrance.

Ownership: NGPC (402) 755-2284

Size: 830 acres

Closest town: Ponca

Cardinals, once rare in western Nebraska, can now be seen across the state. These colorful birds have been able to take advantage of wooded river corridors, tree plantings, and the popularity of winter bird feeding. JACK CURRAN

3. GROVE LAKE WILDLIFE MANAGEMENT AREA

Description: An area of rolling grassland with deciduous trees along ravines that drain to East Verdigre Creek. The site includes Grove Lake, a small impoundment on the creek. Grove Lake WMA is in the transition zone between what was once tallgrass prairie and mixed-grass prairie.

Viewing Information: There are opportunities here for both grassland and woodland birds—woodpeckers, field sparrows, and eastern bluebirds, for example. During spring and fall migrations, look for ospreys. Hiking and driving the perimeter roads offers fairly good year-round opportunities to view wild turkeys and white-tailed deer along the edges where the trees meet the grassland. There is a trout rearing facility at the site; daily visiting hours are 8 A.M. to 5 P.M. There are campgrounds and boat ramps around the lake and parking lots around the perimeter of the site. Roads are well-maintained gravel.

Directions: From U.S. Highway 20 at the town of Royal in Antelope County, go north 2 miles to the southwest corner of the WMA. The trout rearing facility is 1 mile south and 1.5 miles east.

Ownership: NGPC (402) 370-3374

Size: 2,000 acres   **Closest town:** Royal

Eastern bluebirds are "cavity nesters," historically nesting in hollows in decaying trees. Habitat loss, pesticide use, and competition from "imported" cavity nesters such as English sparrows limited the range of eastern bluebirds, but manmade nest boxes have done much to bring them back into their former range.
KEN BOUC

4. WOOD DUCK WILDLIFE MANAGEMENT AREA

Description: Wood Duck WMA contains a series of wetlands in old oxbows along the Elkhorn River. The wetland areas—cattail marshes surrounding open water—are mixed with cottonwood floodplain forest and grassy areas planted to native species and food plots. Wood Duck WMA is increasingly used as a migration stopover for puddle ducks such as teal, mallards, and pintails; diving ducks such as redheads and canvasbacks; and snow geese, white-fronted geese, and Canada geese. Swans occasionally use the area, and later in the migration season, pelicans and cormorants can be seen. There is also a chance to view beavers, muskrats, deer, pheasants, and quail.

Viewing Information: Waterfowl move into the area as the weather warms up, usually late March and April. Viewing is good from county roads that overlook the wetlands and on foot via service roads within the WMA. Look for beavers and muskrats in the wetland areas. Woodland birds can be seen throughout the year, and may include indigo buntings, eastern phoebes, and rose-breasted grosbeaks. Other wetlands along the county roads leading to Wood Duck WMA offer good roadside viewing opportunities. There are parking lots around the perimeter of the WMA. *ROADS TO THE SITE MAY BE FLOODED DURING SPRING OR MUDDY AFTER RAINS. USE CAUTION.*

Directions: *From the junction of U.S. highways 275 and 81 in Norfolk, go south on US 81 for 2 miles, turn east on the county road and go 3 miles; turn south for 1 mile, east for 1 mile, south for 1.5 miles, then east 2.5 miles to the WMA.*

Ownership: NGPC (402) 370-3374

Size: 629 acres   **Closest town:** Stanton

Wood ducks, like several other species, have responded well to artificial nest boxes. Their range in Nebraska is limited largely to wooded areas along stream courses. JON FARRAR

Description: The refuge is largely characterized by DeSoto Lake, once a 7-mile-long bend of the Missouri River. Habitats include lake and river shoreline, forested (cottonwood, black willow, box elder) river floodplain, backwaters, wetlands, and grassland planted to native species. Managed primarily as a stopover for migrating ducks and geese, the refuge sees spectacular numbers of snow geese (up to 500,000) and ducks. Bald eagles follow the geese into the area; as many as 100 eagles winter until March. Opportunities are also excellent year-round for white-tailed deer and wild turkeys. Wetlands provide habitat for beavers, muskrats, and minks. Coyotes are often seen, especially during the waterfowl migration, feeding on injured ducks and geese. Bird feeders at the visitor center are popular places to view migrating songbirds.

Viewing Information: The peak for snow goose viewing is during fall migration, usually in late November. Other ducks and geese are on the refuge spring (March and April) and fall (October and November). These are also the best times for viewing bald eagles. The visitor center (open 9 A.M. to 4:30 P.M. daily) and the barrier-free wildlife overlook provide the best opportunities for viewing eagles and waterfowl. White-tailed deer can be viewed year-round, often from roads at dawn and dusk. Parts of the refuge are closed for the benefit of the migrating birds—pick up maps and brochures at the visitor center.

Directions: *From Blair, Nebraska, go 7 miles east on U.S. Highway 30 (crossing the Missouri River bridge) to the refuge entrance.*

Ownership: USFWS (712) 642-4121

Size: 7,823 acres   **Closest town:** Blair

As recently as the 1960s, few snow geese stopped at DeSoto Refuge during the fall migration. But in recent years numbers have increased to an estimated half-million birds. BOB GRIER

6. NEALE WOODS NATURE CENTER

Description: Neale Woods's 554 acres contain many of the habitats once abundant along the Missouri River, including forested floodplain, wooded hillsides, ridges, ravines, and restored prairie. One hundred and ninety species of birds have been identified here. It is a good location to view white-tailed deer and wild turkeys, and wildflowers are abundant along some of the trails. Each year a butterfly garden is planted, attracting common butterflies such as monarchs and swallowtails and sometimes uncommon ones such as regal fritillaries, skippers, and buckeyes.

Viewing Information: Nine miles of marked and well-maintained trails wind through forests and prairie, some gently sloped and others fairly steep. A brochure with trail descriptions is available at the interpretive center, along with other interpretive materials and bird lists. Deer can be seen year-round. Wild turkeys nest at the site and are best seen in winter and spring. Other nesters at Neale Woods include turkey vultures, red-tailed hawks, screech owls, great horned owls, barred owls, and a number of woodpeckers. The spring songbird migration peaks in May.

Directions: *North of Omaha, take the 30th Street exit (13) off Interstate 680, turn south on 30th St., then immediately left (east) on Dick Collins Road. Continue 0.25 mile to Pershing Drive and turn left (north). Continue 2.7 miles, then turn left onto White Deer Lane. Take the first left onto Edith Marie Avenue. Neale Woods is 0.25 mile ahead.*

Ownership: Fontenelle Forest Association (402) 453-5615

Size: 554 acres   **Closest town:** Omaha

P 🔖 🚶 $

There are seven species of swallowtail butterflies in Nebraska. Among the flowers most attractive to them are thistles, verbena, phlox, zinnias, dill, and fennel. KEN BOUC

7. FONTENELLE FOREST NATURE CENTER

Description: Though it has a history of other uses, this site has been protected as a forest for more than 80 years. The topography is typical of the landscape along the west bank of the Missouri River—hills and ridges formed by deposits of wind-blown silt (loess) with floodplain forest and marshes below. Forty species of broadleaf trees survive here, dominated on the ridges by bur oak, shagbark hickory, and basswood and below by hackberry, black walnut, mulberry, and cottonwood. More than 250 species of birds can be viewed here, and it is a premier site for white-tailed deer and smaller mammals such as raccoons, beavers, minks, opossums, coyotes, and foxes. Marshes in the floodplain provide excellent viewing of water birds. During summer look for red-shouldered hawks and wood ducks. During spring migration, look for rose-breasted grosbeaks and many types of warblers. Fontenelle Forest provides some of the northernmost eastern deciduous forest habitat for species such as the gray squirrel.

Viewing Information: There are more than 17 miles of well-marked and maintained trails in Fontenelle Forest, including a 1-mile-long barrier-free boardwalk with interpretive signs at key areas. Please stay on the trails to minimize the impact on soil and plants. Viewing is excellent from the boardwalk—animals seem to treat viewers along it as part of the scenery. A photography/observation blind offers close-up viewing over a marsh. Trail maps and bird and mammal lists are available at the interpretive center (open 8 A.M. to 5 P.M. daily). On weekends and with advance arrangement, the site offers naturalist-led hikes and other educational programs. For waterfowl, visit during migrations, especially October and November. For songbirds, deer, beavers, and muskrats, visit year-round. Best times are mornings and especially evenings.

Directions: South of Omaha in Bellevue, take the U.S. Highway 75 exit from Interstate 80; go south on US 75 for 2.5 miles to the Chandler Blvd. exit. Turn left (east) on Chandler until it ends at Bellevue Blvd. Turn right on Bellevue; Fontenelle Forest is 0.5 mile ahead on the left.

Ownership: Fontenelle Forest Association (402) 731-3140

Size: 1,311 acres   **Closest town:** Bellevue

> ***Southern flying squirrels can be found only in the southeastern corner of Nebraska. Their habitat is in the oak-hickory forest along the Missouri River and its tributaries. They are very rarely seen because of their strictly nocturnal habits.***

Yellow warblers are common spring and fall migrants and nesters in Nebraska. They prefer wet habitats—look for them along the brushy edges of creeks and marshes. JON FARRAR

8. RANDALL W. SCHILLING WILDLIFE AREA

Description: Managed mostly for waterfowl, the Schilling area overlooks the confluence of the Missouri and Platte rivers. The primary viewing opportunities are for snow geese during fall migration, when more than 200,000 birds can be on the site. Canada, Ross's, and white-fronted geese, as well as ducks (mostly mallards) also use the area.

Viewing Information: Access to Schilling is as follows: From April 1 to Oct. 15, open 7 A.M. to 9 P.M. by vehicle along area access roads. From Nov. 1 to Dec. 15, by guided tour each Sunday at 4 P.M. if geese are on the site (be there at 4 P.M. with your vehicle). From Jan. 1 to March 31, foot access only. Contact the area manager for special group tours.

Directions: From the east edge of Plattsmouth, go 1 mile north on the county road to the site.

Ownership: NGPC (402) 298-8041

Size: 1,500 acres   **Closest town:** Plattsmouth

9. SCHRAMM PARK STATE RECREATION AREA AND AK-SAR-BEN AQUARIUM OUTDOOR EDUCATION CENTER

Description: A day-use recreation area set in the bluffs overlooking the Platte River, and an aquarium displaying a cross-section of the aquatic species found in Nebraska's lakes and streams. The park offers, in a small area, the range of Platte River habitats, from bare sandbars to oak-dominated upland forest. Viewing opportunities include woodland mammals, waterfowl on the area's ponds, songbirds, and a rare opportunity to hear whip-poor-wills. The aquarium and education center feature more than 50 species of aquatic life, including the endangered pallid sturgeon and threatened lake sturgeon.

Viewing Information: The education center serves as the focal point of activities, with displays and educational material. The recreation area is day-use only (dawn to dusk year-round) with 3 miles of trails that start on the floodplain and move up into the upland forest. Summer is best for songbirds. Some waterfowl are here year-round, along with white-tailed deer and turkeys. The aquarium is open year-round, but hours change seasonally. Check with the aquarium at the phone number below.

Directions: From Interstate 80 between Lincoln and Omaha, take Exit 432 (Nebraska Highway 31) and go south 6 miles to the site.

Ownership: NGPC (402) 332-3901

Size: 330 acres   **Closest town:** Gretna

Description: Overlooking the Platte River, park habitats include eastern deciduous forests on hilly uplands and steep creek drainages, floodplain deciduous forest, and areas of open grassland. The site offers good opportunities to view white-tailed deer and wild turkeys in the upland forest and along the edges of the grassy areas. Songbirds typical of this area include scarlet tanagers, ovenbirds, and wood thrushes.

Viewing Information: Bird lists and maps of more than 10 miles of hiking trails are available at the park office. The park is a popular recreation area in the summer, but during the migration periods (May and September/October) it is much less crowded. Two observation towers overlook the Platte River and woodlands. Cabins and tipis can be rented at the park. The nearest camping is 4 miles away at Louisville State Recreation Area.

Directions: *From the junction of Nebraska highways 66 and 50 at Louisville, go 2 miles west on NE 66 to the park entrance.*

Ownership: NGPC (402) 234-2217

Size: 418 acres   **Closest town:** Louisville

Wild turkeys were reintroduced in Nebraska beginning in 1959. They now occur statewide in wooded areas. A popular way to bring turkeys into photography range is by imitating a turkey's various yelps and calls. BOB GRIER

11. JACK SINN MEMORIAL WILDLIFE MANAGEMENT AREA

Description: Once locally abundant, saline wetlands such as this one have largely disappeared due to commercial, residential, and agricultural development. Up to 70 percent of the area is seasonally wet. Typical vegetation in these wet areas are salt-tolerant species such as saltgrass, spearscale, marshelder, and narrow-leaf cattail. During spring and fall migrations, the site features many different ducks, including mallards, blue-winged teal, gadwalls, wigeons, shovelers, and pintails. Common shorebirds and wading birds include rails, dowitchers, snipe, killdeer, and yellowlegs. During winter look for short-eared owls, which, unlike most owls, are often active during the day. The site is also good for sedge wrens, red-winged blackbirds, minks, and muskrats.

Viewing Information: Waterfowl viewing is easiest from the parking lot overlooking an open-water area just east of U.S. Highway 77 south of Ceresco. Much of the site is wet—boots or waders are useful. An abandoned rail line offers dry walking-access from the parking lot on the county road west of US 77. Best times to visit are the migration periods for good numbers of ducks and shorebirds.

Directions: From Ceresco, go 1 mile south on U.S. Highway 77. Turn east on the gravel road and drive to the parking lot. Other parking lots are located throughout the area; watch for signs.

Ownership: NGPC (402) 471-5558

Size: 1,023 acres   **Closest town:** Ceresco

Short-eared owls live in open grassland and marshes and frequently hunt on bright sunny days. Like other owls, short-eared owls eat mostly rodents such as mice and meadow voles. KEN BOUC

Description: A 1,800-acre reservoir surrounded by rolling hills. Once predominantly grassland, the area contains native tree stands (cottonwood, green ash, elm, cedar, and oak) in wooded draws, and tree plantings of cedar, pine, and various shrubs that are now mature. Of particular interest here are waterfowl during spring and fall migrations. An estimated 50,000 to 100,000 snow geese stopped here during the spring of 1996. Look for migrating bald eagles early fall and winter and white pelicans and cormorants in secluded bays and coves during spring migration. Watch for deer and Canada geese year-round and an occasional loon or osprey spring and fall.

Viewing Information: Wildlife lands and parking lots surround the lake. The southwest corner of the WMA is set aside as a waterfowl refuge during waterfowl hunting season; it is closed to hunting but open to walking access. Signs indicate the refuge area. Gravel roads within the WMA lead to parking areas overlooking the lake, offering good waterfowl viewing during migration periods. Look for white-tailed deer at dawn and dusk near the edges of tree plantings and along the roads. The best time for pelicans and cormorants is late April and May. The area receives heavy recreational use, especially in summer. Park entry permits are required for some areas.

Directions: *From the junction of U.S. Highway 34 and Nebraska Highway 79 northwest of Lincoln, turn north on NE 79 and drive 5 miles to the flashing red light (Raymond Road). Turn left (west) on Raymond and go 3 miles to Branched Oak Lake.*

Ownership: COE and NGPC, managed by NGPC (402) 471-5558

Size: 3,961 upland, 1,800 water acres   **Closest town:** Raymond

Canada geese are adaptable birds. With transplanting programs and artificial nesting structures, they have increased their breeding range in Nebraska to some Sandhills lakes, the North Platte and Platte rivers, and ponds and lakes in southeastern Nebraska. DON CUNNINGHAM

EASTERN

29

13. NINE-MILE PRAIRIE

Description: This tract of tallgrass prairie has been studied since the 1920s. The generally rolling terrain alternates with ravines, providing local relief of more than 100 feet. Warm-season, native tall grasses, numerous legumes, goldenrods, asters, and sunflowers blanket the prairie. Cottonwood, willow, green ash, and hackberry are the principal trees dominating natural drainages. Published records indicate that 400-plus species of plants have been collected, observed, or photographed here since the 1920s.

Viewing Information: The most common breeding birds here are ground-nesting species such as western meadowlarks, grasshopper sparrows, upland sandpipers, and bobolinks. Red-tailed hawks, great horned owls, and northern harriers can be seen year-round. Every spring, watch for migrating warblers in wooded ravines and shrub clumps. Larger mammals include coyotes, badgers, white-tailed deer, and raccoons. Typical smaller mammals include prairie voles and 13-lined ground squirrels. The regal fritillary is a relatively common sight from late spring to mid-summer, as are monarch and yellow swallowtail butterflies, cicadas, tiger beetles, katydids, dragonflies, and a variety of ants. Summer wildflowers such as leadplants and prairie coneflowers dot the prairie with color. An autumn visual bonus is the deep blue prairie gentian.

Directions: *From the intersection of NW 48th Street and West Fletcher Avenue on the west edge of Lincoln, go approximately 0.75 mile west to the site.*

Ownership: University of Nebraska Foundation

Size: 230 acres   **Closest town:** Lincoln

Upland sandpipers are grassland birds often seen calling from fenceposts or rock piles. They arrive in Nebraska in April and are usually gone by late July.
KEN BOUC

30

Description: With the goal of representing most of Nebraska's diverse habitats, this nature center has small areas of riparian woodlands, saline wetland, marsh, and tallgrass prairies. Two hundred thirty-seven species of birds have been identified here, 49 species of mammals, and many reptiles and amphibians. Birds include woodland and grassland species and wetland birds such as great blue herons and resident and migrating ducks and geese.

Viewing Information: There are two interpretive centers and more than 6 miles of hiking trails through all of the center's habitats. A bridge spans a saline creek that flows through the site, and boardwalks allow visitors to walk through a marsh. Large windows within the Chet Ager building overlook a bird garden. There are exhibit herds of bison, elk, and white-tailed deer which can be easily viewed from the trails. The two buildings and some trails are barrier-free. The buildings contain animal exhibits and activities for children. Some of the trails have interpretive signs; brochures for other trails are available (as well as bird lists, maps, and activities information) at both buildings. The nature center can also direct you to other nearby prairie areas.

Directions: *In Lincoln, take Nebraska Highway 77 to West Van Dorn Street. Turn west on Van Dorn to Coddington Avenue; turn south on Coddington and go 0.25 mile to the entrance to Pioneers Park. Follow the nature center signs to the center parking area in the southwest corner of Pioneers Park.*

Ownership: City of Lincoln (402) 441-7895

Size: 192 acres

Closest town: Lincoln

Great blue herons are commonly spotted foraging in shallows along lake shores, marshes, and streams. They feed on fish and frogs, spearing them with thrusts of their long, sharp bills.
ROCKY HOFFMANN

31

15. WILDERNESS PARK

Description: A 7-mile-long linear park along Salt Creek at the southwest edge of Lincoln. The park features diverse habitats, primarily mixed-hardwood forest (bur oak, ash, black walnut, hackberry, and basswood) along with small areas of prairie and once-cleared fields in various successional stages of regrowth. Common wildlife species include red foxes, raccoons, coyotes, striped skunks, and ground squirrels. Spring through fall look for catbirds, brown thrashers, goldfinches, field sparrows, red-tailed hawks, and kestrels. Listen for great horned and screech owls. The peak of the songbird migration is in May; look for warblers, vireos, flycatchers, orioles, and grosbeaks.

Viewing Information: The park offers a variety of viewing opportunities, including a day camp area used for environmental education (contact Pioneers Park Nature Center for information), an environmental study area (between Calvert Street and Old Cheney Road), and more than 20 miles of hiking, biking, and horseback trails. There are six parking lots within and around the park, with trailheads at each of them. The prime bird watching areas are between West Old Cheney Road and Saltillo Road. It is best to visit in low-use times (early morning or winter). The park is used less in its southern portions.

Directions: *The day camp parking area and Epworth Environmental Study Area parking are off Nebraska Highway 77 via Van Dorn Street. Turn east on Van Dorn to Park Blvd.; turn south on 1st Street to the parking lots. For the other lots, from NE 77 follow either Pioneers Blvd., Old Cheney Road, 14th Street, or Saltillo Road.*

Ownership: City of Lincoln (402) 441-7895

Size: 1,455 acres   **Closest town:** Lincoln

Red foxes will make use of old badger burrows, hollow logs, or even culverts as denning sites, and will eat whatever they can catch, from mice to grasshoppers and beetles. ROCKY HOFFMANN

16. INDIAN CAVE STATE PARK

Description: Indian Cave State Park is an extension of the eastern deciduous forest more typical of places south and east of Nebraska; thus it features habitats and species that are unusual to the state. The landscape is typical of this part of the Missouri River—bluffs formed by wind-blown silt (loess); steep cuts to the Missouri River floodplain; and floodplain forest, marshes, and backwaters. The park offers excellent opportunities to view deer, wild turkeys, woodchucks, beavers, and raccoons. It also offers the rare opportunity to see gray squirrels in Nebraska. There are flying squirrels in the park but sightings are rare. You may hear bobcats. Indian Cave is also an excellent birding spot.

Viewing Information: Slowly driving the upper park roads at dawn is a reliable way to view deer and wild turkeys; along the lower roads near the river look for woodchucks and shorebirds. There are 20 miles of hiking trails that wind up and down through the park's various habitats, offering the best opportunities for birding. Of particular interest might be barred owls, tanagers, hairy and red-headed woodpeckers, and whip-poor-wills in spring and summer. The park is a good spot for black rat snakes (a rarity in other parts of Nebraska) and occasional timber rattlers. Some of the trails are steep; check with the park office for trail information and unusual viewing opportunities.

Directions: *From the junction of U.S. Highway 136 and Nebraska Highway 67 at Brownville, go south to Nebraska Spur 64E (approximately 9 miles). Turn east and drive 5 miles to the park.*

Ownership: NGPC (402) 883-2575

Size: 3,000 acres   **Closest town:** Shubert

Indian Cave State Park contains the largest area of eastern deciduous forest in public ownership in Nebraska. Fall foliage offers one of the showiest displays of color in the state. KEN BOUC

Description: A small impoundment surrounded by gently rolling native tallgrass prairie and one of the best examples of tallgrass prairie in public ownership. Tall grasses include big bluestem, Indian grass, little bluestem, and switchgrass. Forbs include white prairie clover, leadplant, prairie rose, and goldenrod. There is a prairie chicken "booming ground" here, and it is a good place to see grassland birds such as upland sandpipers, grasshopper sparrows, meadowlarks, and dickcissels. Burchard Lake is also a stopover spot for waterfowl during the migration. There are massasauga rattlesnakes here (small rattlesnakes that live in wetter tallgrass prairies).

Viewing Information: Wildflowers bloom throughout the summer and into early fall. March and April are the premier times for waterfowl and prairie chicken viewing at Burchard Lake. Two observation blinds have been set up near the prairie chicken booming ground and are available on a first-come, first-served basis. Locate the blinds the day before you want to use them; the birds begin their display before dawn, and you must be in the blind well before sunrise to avoid disturbing the birds. Burchard Lake is a waterfowl refuge during waterfowl hunting seasons, and access to the area is closed.

Directions: *From the junction of Nebraska highways 99 and 4 north of Burchard, go 3 miles east, and then 1.5 miles south on the county road to the site.*

Ownership: NGPC (402) 471-5558

Size: 560 acres (150 lake)   **Closest town:** Burchard

When searching for muskrats, look over the marsh for their cone-shaped houses made of cattails or bulrush. The presence of muskrats is often taken as an indicator of the health and vigor of wetlands. DON CUNNINGHAM

Description: Pawnee Prairie is a good site for grassland birds such as grasshopper sparrows, meadowlarks, and prairie chickens. The WMA contains a greater prairie chicken lek—an area where year after year male greater prairie chickens perform their breeding display. For greater prairie chickens this display is called "booming" and the area is called a "booming ground." Ponds created to slow drainage toward Johnson Creek attract mallards and teal in the spring and summer. This is also a site for massasauga rattlesnakes.

Viewing Information: The prairie chicken booming ground (used yearly by 15 to 20 birds) is near the center of the area (a 0.75-mile hike from any of the parking lots), but no permanent blinds have been established. You are welcome to put up a temporary blind. Parking lots surround the site, but no vehicles are allowed on the area. The peak of the prairie chicken activity is in late March and April.

Directions: From the junction of Nebraska highways 99 and 8, 6 miles south of Burchard, turn east on the county road and go 1 mile to northwest corner of the site. Gravel roads surround the area; other parking lots are on the east side of the site and the southwest corner.

Ownership: NGPC (402) 471-5558

Size: 1,120 acres   **Closest town:** Burchard

EASTERN

Prairie chickens favor areas that are largely native grassland interspersed with cropland. They are most numerous in Nebraska along the eastern and southern edge of the Sandhills. The spring courtship display of prairie chickens is a popular wildlife viewing attraction in Nebraska. ROCKY HOFFMANN

Description: This 160-acre tract was one of the first in the nation to be claimed under the Homestead Act of 1862. Established as a national monument in 1936, Homestead was one of the first places within the national park system to attempt the restoration of a native prairie. Hardwood forest along Cub Creek adds to the habitat diversity. More than 150 bird species have been identified here, including common grassland nesters such as meadowlarks and dickcissels; hawks, particularly red-tailed hawks; and many migrants. Viewers along Homestead's trails have reported deer, beavers, foxes, wild turkeys, pheasants, and badgers.

Viewing Information: Self-guided walking trails loop through both the forested and prairie parts of the area. Brochures are available at the visitor center, along with bird lists, plant lists, historical information about the site, and information about tallgrass prairie and restoration efforts. Signs along the trails help interpret the site. A native plant display helps identify grasses and forbs.

Directions: *From the junction of U.S. Highway 136 and Nebraska Highway 4 in Beatrice, go west on NE 4 for 3.5 miles to the visitor center.*

Ownership: NPS (402) 223-3514

Size: 160 acres   **Closest town:** Beatrice

Meadowlarks are found year-round in Nebraska. They are perhaps the most popular of grassland birds; six states, including Nebraska, have made the meadowlark their state bird. KEN BOUC

Description: Meridian WMA features woodlands and former cropland planted to grass on the floodplain of the Little Blue River, rising into steep draws forested in oak and ash and finally native grassland above. The site offers opportunities to view both woodland and grassland species of birds—eastern bluebirds, flycatchers, orioles, and wood thrushes—and the deer and turkeys that are familiar in almost all areas of Nebraska. Rocky ledges in the wooded draws harbor bobcats, but they are extremely elusive. Look on area ponds for wood ducks. The grasslands in the northeast corner are good for viewing prairie wildflowers (blazing star, coneflowers, heath asters, and compass plants) in spring and summer.

Viewing Information: Access within the WMA is on foot from parking lots around the perimeter and from the county road that cuts through the middle. Mowed service roads provide hiking trails through most of the habitats on the WMA. Spring and summer are best for songbirds and wildflowers.

Directions: *From Alexandria, go approximately 1.75 miles south on Nebraska Highway 53; turn west on the county road that follows the Blue River approximately 1 mile to Meridian WMA.*

Ownership: NGPC (402) 749-7650

Size: 400 acres   **Closest town:** Alexandria

The reclusive and nocturnal habits of the bobcat, Nebraska's most common native cat, make them difficult animals to watch and photograph. They prefer rugged canyonlands or densely timbered areas like those along river bottoms.
DON CUNNINGHAM

REGION 2: SOUTH-CENTRAL NEBRASKA

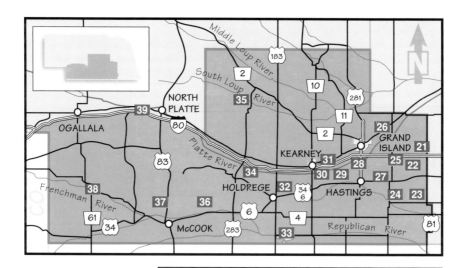

Wildlife Viewing Sites

21. Kirkpatrick North Wildlife Management Area
22. Rainwater Basin Auto Tour
23. Mallard Haven Waterfowl Production Area
24. Massie Waterfowl Production Area
25. Pintail Wildlife Management Area
26. Bader Memorial Park Natural Area
27. Harvard Waterfowl Production Area
28. Mormon Island Crane Meadows
29. Crane Meadows Nature Center
30. Lillian Annette Rowe Sanctuary
31. Fort Kearny Hike-Bike Trail/Bassway Strip Wildlife Management Area
32. Funk Waterfowl Production Area
33. Harlan County Reservoir
34. Johnson No. 2 Hydroplant
35. Pressey Wildlife Management Area
36. Medicine Creek Wildlife Management Area
37. Red Willow Reservoir
38. Enders Reservoir
39. North River Wildlife Management Area

Description: Easily visible from Interstate 80, Kirkpatrick North WMA gets its share of attention. In spring, it's because the site attracts thousands of migrating blue-winged teal, pintails, northern shovelers, and snow geese. In summer and fall, attention turns to one of the management techniques used—short-term, intensive grazing to recreate habitat disturbances once caused by bison. Kirkpatrick is managed primarily to provide a rich food supply for migrating waterfowl; grazing and trampling, particularly on the wetland edge and transition zone between wetlands and uplands, creates openings in what would otherwise be a solid stand of vegetation. As the water recedes throughout the summer, seed-producing plants invade. The seeds eventually provide carbohydrate-rich food for migrating birds during fall and the following spring.

Viewing Information: The best time to view migrating waterfowl is in late February and March. Late March through early June is good for shorebirds such as American avocets, dowitchers, and sandpipers. The wetland edge is grazed during the summer. Other areas are grazed at other times to accomplish other management goals. For example, areas that contain cool-season (spring and fall) non-native grasses such as bluegrass and brome are grazed when they are most vigorous. The goal is to reduce their density and to encourage the growth of native, warm-season grasses.

Directions: From Interstate 80, take exit 348 (6 miles west of York); go north on the county road 0.5 mile, turn east, and go 1 mile more to the site.

Ownership: NGPC (308) 865-5310

Size: 160 acres   **Closest town:** York

SOUTH-CENTRAL

Mallards are among the most common migrating ducks in Nebraska. Typical "dabbling" ducks, mallards' feet are set more forward on their bodies than on diving ducks. They feed by tipping up, with only their tails showing above the water. JON FARRAR

Description: This auto tour gives drivers an opportunity to see many of the best of the wetland areas in the eastern part of the Rainwater Basin. (Some of these wetlands are described in more detail as individual sites.) The auto tour provides an overlook of these areas and an opportunity to see the basins as "islands" or "oases" in a landscape that is intensively farmed. Rainwater Basin Waterfowl Production Areas and Wildlife Management Areas are managed primarily as staging areas for migrating ducks and geese in the spring. Concentrations of birds in February and March are astonishing. These sites are also invaluable for wading birds and shorebirds, including the endangered whooping crane, from March through mid-June.

Viewing Information: The auto tour can be a long drive if you linger at any of the 12 WPAs and WMAs. The tour passes through several small towns where facilities are available. Several of the wetlands—Mallard Haven, Eckhardt, and Pintail—offer good roadside viewing and parking lots are available without turning off the tour route. Many of the tour roads are all-weather gravel; roads within the WPAs and WMAs may not be passable. Bring your binoculars or a spotting scope for the best roadside/parking lot viewing. Mornings and evenings are best for the largest concentrations of birds.

Directions: *Follow the map below to take the auto tour. The complete tour is 112 miles—allow enough time. Begin the tour from Interstate 80 at the York exit (353) to take the tour from east to west; or start from I-80 at the Aurora exit (332) to take the tour west to east.*

Ownership: USFWS (308) 236-5015; NGPC (308) 865-5310; Rainwater Basin Joint Venture (308) 385-6465

Size: 112 miles   **Closest Towns:** York; Aurora

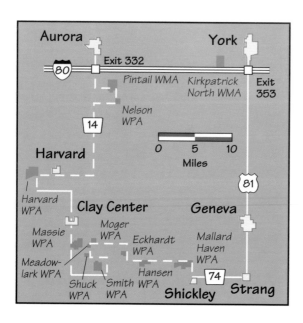

23. MALLARD HAVEN WATERFOWL PRODUCTION AREA

Description: One of the larger Rainwater Basins, Mallard Haven WPA has a good mix of semipermanent wetlands (wet most of the time), seasonal wetlands (areas that are wet in spring and early summer but dry out as the weather warms), and grassland that is being restored to native species.

Viewing Information: In late February and March, Mallard Haven provides habitat for thousands of white-fronted geese and snow geese and nearly 20 species of ducks. Great blue herons, snowy egrets, and many shorebirds use the area late March through mid-June. Breeding wetland birds include yellow-headed blackbirds, red-winged blackbirds, northern harriers, and great-tailed grackles. Mammals such as muskrats, minks, and white-tailed deer can also be seen at Mallard Haven. There are parking areas around the perimeter of the site and an information kiosk at the southeast parking lot.

Directions: *From Nebraska Highway 74 at Shickley, turn north on the county road and go 1.25 miles to the entrance road to the information kiosk at the southeast corner of the site.*

Ownership: USFWS (308) 236-5015

Size: 1,087 acres   **Closest town:** Shickley

24. MASSIE WATERFOWL PRODUCTION AREA

Description: One of several Rainwater Basin wetlands in which water levels can be maintained by pumping groundwater—a method of sustaining habitat despite decreasing numbers of wetlands and year-to-year fluctuations in water levels. During migrations, Massie WPA attracts large numbers of shorebirds, wading birds, geese, and ducks. Wetland birds such as loggerhead shrikes, eastern and western flycatchers, and bobolinks nest here. It is a good site for muskrats—look for their lodges along the edges of open water.

Viewing Information: Recently the community of Clay Center built an observation blind that provides a good overlook of both open water and river bulrush marsh. The blind is located about 200 feet from the parking lot on the south side of Massie WPA. There is also an information kiosk here. The road to this parking lot is graveled and is passable; roads to other parking lots around the perimeter of the area are driveable only in dry weather.

Directions: *From the junction of Nebraska highways 14 and 41 in Clay Center, go south 4 miles on NE 14; turn left (east) on the gravel road, go 1 mile, and turn left again (north) to the kiosk parking lot.*

Ownership: USFWS (308) 236-5015

Size: 853 acres   **Closest town:** Clay Center

Description: Another basin with a mix of habitats. Some are wet almost all the time, some dry out as the season warms, and some are uplands. Trees—primarily cedar—and shrubs have been planted to provide winter food and cover for upland birds. This marsh has historically been a favorite stopover for northern pintails and white-fronted geese.

Viewing Information: Pintail has large concentrations of ducks and geese in late February and March; shorebird viewing is best March through May. A new parking lot on the east side of the site provides good access to the marsh and the open water; walk the old service road to the water's edge. Old duck-hunting dugouts overlooking the marsh from the southwest corner can be used as viewing blinds. Look for pheasants, northern harriers, and migrating peregrine falcons on the uplands.

Directions: *From Interstate 80 at the Aurora exit (332) go south on Nebraska Highway 14 for 1.5 miles. Turn left (east) on the county road and go 3 miles; turn south on the county road and go 1 mile to the east parking lot at Pintail WMA. Walk 0.25 mile to the water's edge.*

Ownership: NGPC (308) 865-5310

Size: 478 acres   **Closest town:** Aurora

Pintails, along with mallards, are the earliest spring migrants to Nebraska. Some stay to breed in the Rainwater Basin and the Sandhills. As egg laying begins, pintail drakes pursue the hens of other mated pairs, resulting in nests being distributed over wide areas. JON FARRAR

Description: A small reserve along the Platte River that has been described as a microcosm of the Platte River. The natural area includes a stretch of the Platte River, floodplain woodlands, sandpits, and tallgrass prairie. The river and ponds here are used by migrating ducks and geese beginning in February and peaking in March. Occasionally the site is also used by sandhill cranes. Mudflats and sandbars in the river are used by shorebirds and waders—least sandpipers, great blue herons, and great egrets—especially during spring and summer. The floodplain woods are a mix of trees and shrubs dominated by cottonwoods and are home to more typically eastern species such as house wrens, vireos, yellow warblers, cardinals, and American woodcocks. It is a good area to see deer and raccoons. Weasels and minks are present but elusive—look for their tracks. The tallgrass prairie is home to many birds (meadowlarks, bobolinks, dickcissels, and grasshopper sparrows) and insects (painted lady and regal fritillary butterflies and a variety of beetles).

Viewing Information: Trails have been developed around and through all of the major habitat types in Bader Park. You are also welcome to go into these areas and experience them close up. Bring binoculars for looking across the river at the sandbars and into the treetops for birds, and take the time to look on the milkweeds for beetles or on the meadow violets for regal fritillaries. *LOWLAND AREAS ARE USUALLY WET IN SPRING. BE AWARE OF PLANTS SUCH AS POISON IVY AND STINGING NETTLES.*

Directions: *From U.S. Highway 30 at Grand Island, go east through Chapman to Bader Park Road; turn south and go 3 miles to the park.*

Ownership: Bader Park Board

Size: 80 acres

Closest town: Chapman

Minks are members of the weasel family, along with otters and skunks. Minks make their homes in natural cavities in stream banks under trees and drift piles; often they will use abandoned muskrat lodges and burrows. Although they live in wetland areas, they are not as well adapted for swimming as beavers or muskrats. JON FARRAR

Description: A mecca for migrating waterfowl and shorebirds, with open water during most years, moist-soil wetlands (areas where the soil is water-saturated), and grassland that is being restored to native species. Harvard is a large area, mostly treeless, and provides a rare opportunity to get a feel for what a presettlement landscape might have been like. Harvard is an excellent viewing site for white-fronted geese, snow geese, pintails, and ruddy ducks during late February and March and from October through November. It is also excellent for stilt, pectoral, and spotted sandpipers and semipalmated plovers from March to mid-June. Breeding birds include short-eared owls, common yellowthroats, and northern harriers. You may see bald eagles or black terns in February and March.

Viewing Information: Harvard is a good place to get out and walk. There is an information kiosk at the southwest parking lot, and from there a 2-mile hiking trail goes along a dike, passes through semi-permanent and moist-soil wetlands, and through tallgrass prairie. A winter walk is likely to turn up roosts of 10 to 15 short-eared owls; most other birds are viewed during migrations. Other parking lots are located around the perimeter of the site.

Directions: *From the junction of U.S. Highway 6 and Nebraska Highway 14 north of Clay Center, go west on US 6 for 8 miles. Turn north on the gravel road, go 2 miles, turn right, and go east to the information kiosk parking lot.*

Ownership: USFWS (308) 236-5015

Size: 1,484 acres   **Closest town:** Harvard

The importance of wetlands in south-central Nebraska to white-fronted geese cannot be overstated. Some 80 percent of the mid-continent population of these birds stages in Nebraska during the spring migration—as many as 200,000 birds.
JON FARRAR

Description: An extensive area of wet meadows and tallgrass prairie adjacent to the Platte River, this site hosts high densities of sandhill cranes, ducks, and geese during the spring migration. As many as 70,000 cranes have been observed foraging on the wet meadows, and more than 80,000 birds have roosted in the adjacent river in late March and early April. The site's bird list now stands at 223 species. May through August is peak time for grassland birds such as upland sandpipers, dickcissels, bobolinks, grasshopper sparrows, and sedge wrens, all of which nest here. Look for bald eagles in winter and great horned owls year-round.

Viewing Information: During crane season, viewing of this area is limited to roadside viewing along Elm Island Road. Pull as far off the road as possible to avoid causing traffic problems; many people are out on these roads during crane season. At other times, walking access is allowed *(YOU MUST CALL FOR PERMISSION)* on the area. All the property adjacent to Elm Island Road and west of where the road dead ends is Crane Trust property. Park along the Elm Island Road and walk along the private road that goes down along the river.

Directions: *From Interstate 80, take the U.S. Highway 281 exit (312) and go south 1 mile to Elm Island Road. Turn west, and park along the road.*

Ownership: Platte River Whooping Crane Maintenance Trust (308) 384-4633

Size: 2,500 acres   **Closest town:** Doniphan

It is said that sandhill cranes have been in Nebraska for 10 million years. The Platte River is a critical spring staging area for the birds. During the fall migration, however, flocks of birds are distributed nearly statewide, and they spend little time on the ground. MIKE FORSBERG

Description: The nature center sits on 240 acres of prairie, wet meadows, and riparian forest located between two channels of the Platte River. The center is in the region of the central Platte that is a critical migration stopover for sandhill cranes and waterfowl. Nearby sandbars provide nesting habitat for least terns and piping plovers. Regal fritillary butterflies, smooth green snakes, white-tailed deer, coyotes, and badgers are all common at the center. More than 200 species of birds have been seen here, including bluebirds, magpies, bobolinks, wild turkeys, orchard orioles, and upland sandpipers.

Viewing Information: Crane Meadows Nature Center is a year-round educational organization dedicated to providing insight and access into the ecosystem of the Platte River Valley. An interpretive center located on-site provides displays and information for the public along with a classroom for programs. Naturalists conduct informative nature-related programs and hikes on a year-round basis, and trails are open all year for public hiking. The nature center has 7 miles of hiking trails available to the public from 8:30 A.M. to 5:30 P.M. year-round. Trail maps and wildlife lists are available. During the crane season, the center leases a 25-person observation bunker for sunrise and sunset tours. Call for reservations and costs.

Directions: *From Interstate 80 in central Nebraska, take the Alda exit (305) and go south 0.5 mile on Alda Road (Nebraska Link 40C). The nature center is on the east side of the road.*

Ownership: Crane Meadows Nature Center (308) 382-1820

Size: 240 acres   **Closest town:** Alda

The least tern nests on bare sandbars in the channel of the Platte. Decreasing flows in the Platte have allowed woody vegetation to encroach into the open channel, threatening the survival of these rare birds. JON FARRAR

Description: Managed to preserve the wide river channel, naked sandbars, and shallow water favored as roosting habitat by migrating sandhill cranes, the sanctuary attracts huge numbers of birds during the spring. Numbers of cranes in and around the sanctuary are estimated at 60,000. A quarter or more of the sanctuary (the area north of the river) is grassland, much of it native mid-grass and tallgrass prairie. The prairie in bloom features wildflowers such as coneflowers, black-eyed susans, and poppy mallow, and is home to dickcissels, bobolinks, and regal fritillary butterflies. A birding trail starts from the office.

Viewing Information: Access to the sanctuary is on foot only. During the crane viewing season (March 10 through April 10), observation blinds are set up and the sanctuary staff conducts tours in the morning and evening; contact the office for information. *ACCESS TO THE VIEWING BLINDS IS BY RESERVATION ONLY.* Another site offering good viewing of cranes feeding in nearby fields and flying to and from river roosts is located 0.5 mile past the office. The office is open 9 A.M. to 5 P.M. Monday through Friday. Visitors must stay on established trails. No dogs are allowed.

Directions: *To office and crane season information center, take the Interstate 80 exit at Gibbon (285) and go south 2 miles. Turn right (west) and go 2 miles on the gravel road to the office—the white farmhouse on the right. Other times: take the Minden (Nebraska Highway 10) exit from I-80; go south on NE 10 to the first gravel road (there is an old railroad car here with an "antiques" sign on it); turn left (east) on the gravel road and go 1.2 miles to a parking lot on your right.*

Ownership: National Audubon Society (308) 468-5282

Size: 1,600 acres   **Closest town:** Gibbon

Rowe Sanctuary was established to protect habitat for sandhill cranes. But the site is important to other species, from grassland birds to butterflies and wildflowers.
JON FARRAR

SOUTH-CENTRAL

47

31. FORT KEARNY HIKE-BIKE TRAIL/BASSWAY STRIP WILDLIFE MANAGEMENT AREA

Description: A 1.8-mile-long converted rail line trail over the middle and north channels of the Platte River leading to Bassway Strip, a wildlife management area featuring wooded river floodplain, small lakes, and sandpits. The Hike-Bike Trail is an excellent place to view migrating sandhill cranes (March 10 through April 10) flying overhead as they leave or return to river roosts at dawn and dusk. Other birds to look for on the river are white-fronted, Canada, and snow geese; mallard and pintail ducks; and semipalmated plovers, Baird's sandpipers, and yellowlegs. Wooded areas along the trail and in Bassway Strip may provide opportunities to view northern orioles, vireos, and kingfishers along with white-tailed deer, raccoons, coyotes, pheasants, and wild turkeys.

Viewing Information: Start at the visitor center at Fort Kearny State Historical Park to get information on crane viewing, bird lists, trail information, and a park permit. A trailhead for the Hike-Bike Trail is at Fort Kearny State Recreation Area. The trail crosses two bridges, one of which features observation decks. Kearny SRA has primitive camping near good crane viewing areas.

Directions: *From Kearney, go south on Nebraska Highway 44 across the river to Nebraska Link 50-A. Turn left (east) on Link 50-A and go 4 miles to Fort Kearny State Historical Park. The State Recreation Area is a mile east and a mile north.*

Ownership: NGPC (308) 865-5305

Size: 1.8-mile trail; 729-acre WMA   **Closest town:** Kearney

Northern or "Baltimore" orioles are common over much of Nebraska. Look for them in wooded areas such as riparian cottonwood and willow forests. ROCKY HOFFMANN

48

32. FUNK WATERFOWL PRODUCTION AREA

Description: One of the largest of the Rainwater Basins, and the largest WPA in Nebraska. As with other basins, Funk is a mix of open water, moist-soil wetlands, and grassland replanted to native species. Current thinking is that an "ideal" basin for migrating waterfowl has open water (as much as half its area); shallow wetland areas dominated by plants that waterfowl favor for food (smartweed or wild millet, for example); and is surrounded by upland grassland to provide nesting cover and to buffer the wetland from erosion and siltation. Funk Lagoon is a prime area, hosting hundreds of thousands of geese and twenty species of ducks during spring and fall migrations. In April and October, whooping cranes have stopped here. May through September are good months to view cattle egrets, great blue herons, black-crowned night herons, and common egrets. Thousands of shorebirds stop over here March through May and late July through September. Breeding wetland birds include eared and pied-billed grebes, yellow-headed blackbirds, great-tailed grackles, northern harriers, and common yellowthroats. May through August you may see cinnamon teal and white-faced ibises. Besides birds, Funk is home to muskrats, minks, and white-tailed deer.

Viewing Information: Funk WPA is one of the best Rainwater Basins for wildlife viewing. Parking lots are located around the perimeter of the site, and gravel roads pass by all the different habitats. Funk is an excellent place to walk, featuring a 3-mile loop hiking trail that begins at the central parking lot. The trail passes through semi-permanent and moist-soil wetland areas as well as restored tallgrass prairie. There is an information kiosk at the central parking lot with maps, and an observation blind nearby overlooking open water and cattail marsh. A barrier-free wooden walkway takes you to the blind.

Directions: *From Holdrege, take U.S. Highway 6 east to the town of Funk; turn north at the east edge of Funk and go 2.5 miles; turn east and go 1.1 miles to the kiosk parking lot.*

Ownership: USFWS (308) 236-5015

Size: 1,986 acres   **Closest town:** Funk

The huge spring concentrations of birds that we find so spectacular to view here may, when combined with other factors, actually pose a threat to the birds, mostly from the rapid spread of diseases such as avian cholera. The only long-term solution to the problem is to have more high-quality wetlands to disperse the birds.

33. HARLAN COUNTY RESERVOIR

Description: The largest reservoir and public land area in the Republican River drainage. The landscape varies from wooded creek bed draws to cottonwood-dominated riparian forest to rolling native mixed-grass prairie. Management of the site mixes boundary tree plantings of juniper and red cedar with a mosaic of grass strips and cropped areas. The site offers excellent opportunities to view white-tailed and mule deer; pheasants, quail, and prairie chickens; dabbling ducks and Canada geese; bald eagles; and nesting songbirds. The site is an occasional fall stopover for small numbers of sandhill cranes.

Viewing Information: Paved roads and gravel roads provide good access around the lake. On the north side, drainages to the lake along Methodist and Mill creeks provide good opportunities to view wintering mallards. Roads leading to the edge of the lake provide opportunities to watch wintering bald eagles. An even better site for eagles is east of the south end of the dam, where there is a roost. The eagles stay to take advantage of fish and wintering waterfowl in the open water. In the grassland on the south side of the reservoir are some prairie chicken booming grounds—ask at the Corps of Engineers project office for their locations, or drive the gravel roads and trails on the south side in March and April just before daylight and listen for the distinctive "booming." The south side of the area is best for mule deer, while the north side is best for whitetails. Best places for wild turkeys are on the west end of the area, along the Republican River. There is a prairie dog town at the northeast corner of the site between the administration area and Republican City.

Directions: *Take U.S. Highway 183 south from Holdrege approximately 22 miles to Alma at the west end of Harlan County Reservoir.*

Ownership: COE (308) 799-2105   **Size:** 17,278 acres   **Closest town:** Alma

White pelicans are common migrants through Nebraska. During summer, Harlan County Reservoir and some Sandhills lakes are the best places in the state to view them. JON FARRAR

Description: Bald eagles congregate here during winter to take advantage of open water and easy fishing created by operation of the hydroplant. The turbulence created by the turbine keeps the water below the plant from freezing over and forces fish to the surface. Opportunistic eagles sit in cottonwood trees that overlook the supply canal, watching for fish. The open water also attracts wintering waterfowl.

Viewing Information: The J-2 powerhouse has been modified with large windows and bleachers to accommodate people interested in watching eagles. Spotting scopes are provided for close-up viewing and an attendant is on hand to answer questions. The plant is open for eagle viewing from mid-December until the eagles leave the area. Hours are Saturdays and Sundays 8 A.M. to 2 P.M., and for groups (by appointment only) Thursday and Friday mornings.

Directions: From Lexington, go south on U.S. Highway 283 past Interstate 80; follow signs to the powerhouse (approximately 6 miles).

Ownership: The Central Nebraska Public Power and Irrigation District (308) 995-8601 (Holdredge Office) or (308) 324-2811 (J-2 Hydroplant during hours open for viewing)

Closest town: Lexington

SOUTH-CENTRAL

Bald eagles nested successfully in Nebraska in 1992, the first successful nesting recorded in nearly 100 years. Since then the number of breeding pairs has been steadily increasing in Nebraska.
MIKE FORSBERG

Description: Pressey WMA features riparian forest (cottonwood, willow, boxelder) along the floodplain of the South Loup River; some hand-planted trees (locust, walnut, and a few persimmon); rolling native mixed-grass prairie on the south end of the site; and steep, brushy canyons draining to the river. Pressey WMA is a good viewing area for many species typical of the region—mule deer, white-tailed deer, sharp-tailed grouse, and coyotes. There is a heron rookery on the area with excellent viewing from a wildlife trail. The area offers good birding for both woodland and grassland species. River otters were released at Pressey in an effort to restore them to Nebraska's rivers.

Viewing Information: Pressey WMA is more developed than many WMAs, with camping areas and trails. The wildlife trail along the river passes close to the heron rookery in a cottonwood grove. Hiking the ridges in the rolling prairie provides good viewing of wildlife in the canyons below, especially for mule deer and possibly coyotes. Hiking trails can be accessed from a camping area adjacent to Nebraska Highway 21 or parking lots on the area's perimeter.

Directions: *From Oconto, take Nebraska Highway 21 north 5 miles to Pressey WMA.*

Ownership: NGPC (402) 684-2921

Size: 1,640 acres   **Closest town:** Oconto

River otters were once common in Nebraska. Efforts to restore them to Nebraska's rivers began in 1986. Winter is often the best time to view otters; look for their "slips" or slides in snow along riverbanks. JON FARRAR

Description: This wildlife management area contains grasslands, upland deciduous forest, floodplain forest along Medicine Creek, and wetland areas along the creek and upper end of Medicine Creek Reservoir. The area offers an excellent opportunity to view both white-tailed deer and mule deer year-round; upland birds such as pheasants, quail, and wild turkeys; and waterfowl during the spring and fall migrations. There are usually barn owls here during the spring breeding season, and some years there is a large concentration of wood ducks in August and September.

Viewing Information: Most of Medicine Creek's opportunities are year-round—white-tailed deer, mule deer, turkeys, and pheasants. It is a very popular place to hunt; be sure to check for season openings and closings. The interior roads lead to the best areas. Use trails 13 and 14 to search out concentrations of wood ducks. Best viewing is early or late in the day. Maps are available at the recreation area near the dam. *DO NOT DRIVE INTERIOR ROADS AFTER A RAIN.* There are parking sites throughout the area, although they might not be marked. A park entry permit is required for the recreation area by the dam.

Directions: *From U.S. Highway 34, 2 miles west of Cambridge, go north 7 miles on the county road to Medicine Creek. The site follows the reservoir and Medicine Creek for some 8 miles to the northwest. Good gravel roads take you around the perimeter and give access to interior trails.*

Ownership: USBR, leased to NGPC (308) 535-8025

Size: 7,254 acres   **Closest town:** Cambridge

Mule deer prefer different habitats than white-tailed deer. Classic mule deer habitat is rough—hills and canyons with mixed forest and grassland—where they can use their escape technique of bouncing stiff-legged over the terrain and changing direction unpredictably. Whitetails are hiders, favoring the dense cover along rivers and streams for concealment.
BOB GRIER

SOUTH-CENTRAL

53

Description: A reservoir on Red Willow Creek, surrounded by rolling grass-lands, brushy draws, and tree plantings, mostly cedar and shrubs such as chokecherry and wild plum. Red Willow is one of the best public areas in the state for viewing black-tailed prairie dogs. It is a good site to view white-tailed and mule deer, waterfowl (particularly mallards, pintails, and other dabbling ducks), and occasionally quail and turkeys. It is also a good site to view grass-land and shrub species such as loggerhead shrikes and grasshopper sparrows.

Viewing Information: Best viewing is by driving the interior roads to the reservoir's more remote areas. There are several prairie dog towns around the reservoir; two of the most accessible are at the north end of the Bluegill Arm and near the Spring Creek concession area. Roads are relatively good; some may be impassable in wet weather. Use good judgment. Maps of trails and fa-cilities are available at the concession areas.

Directions: *From McCook, take U.S. Highway 83 north approximately 11 miles to the road to Red Willow Dam. Another road, approximately a mile north, leads to trails on the north side of the reservoir.*

Ownership: USBR, leased to NGPC (308) 535-8025

Size: 6,016 acres   **Closest town:** McCook

Many different species of wildlife are associated with prairie dog towns, among them burrowing owls, which nest in vacant burrows. Grassland birds such as meadowlarks and grasshopper sparrows are attracted to prairie dog towns because seeds and insects are more accessible than they are in the surrounding range land.
JON FARRAR

Description: A reservoir on the Frenchman River surrounded by willows giving way to grassland on the north side. The wildlife lands on the south side of the reservoir are sandsage prairie—hilly and sandy like the Sandhills, but typified by plants (sand sagebrush, for example) found south and southwest of Nebraska. Enders is a good site for white-tailed and mule deer, waterfowl in spring and fall, bald eagles in winter, ornate box turtles in the sandsage prairie, and occasionally wild turkeys. Also in the sandsage prairie look for sagebrush species such as Cassin's sparrows and lark buntings. *THERE ARE PRAIRIE RATTLESNAKES HERE IN ROCKY AREAS ALONG THE RESERVOIR AND IN THE SANDSAGE PRAIRIE.* A portion of the wildlife area is designated a wildlife refuge and is closed to vehicle traffic part of the year.

Viewing Information: Gravel roads and trails give access to more remote areas beyond the recreation facilities near the dam. Access off the gravel and dirt roads is on foot only. The roads are generally driveable but can be impassable in wet weather. Good clearance and four-wheel drive are helpful. The drive through the sandsage prairie along the south side of the reservoir is particularly interesting. Refuge areas are gated and closed October 15 to March 1; hiking is permitted. Maps are available at the concession areas near the dam.

Directions: *From where U.S. Highway 6 and Nebraska Highway 61 join at Imperial, follow these roads 10 miles to the dam.*

Ownership: USBR, leased to NGPC (308) 535-8025

Size: 4,599 acres   **Closest town:** Imperial

The sandsage prairie of southwest Nebraska is different than the sandhills prairie in the north-central part of the state, with a different plant composition.
JON FARRAR

Description: The North Platte River here may seem a different river than the wide, braided central Platte to the east. Here the channel is narrow and heavily wooded. Nonetheless, there is a sandhill crane roost in the less-wooded shallows on the southeast edge of the site—a 0.75-mile hike through brush from the north parking lot. North River has fairly good habitat diversity in a small area, with cottonwood groves; brush (mainly Russian olive); meadows that may or may not be wet, depending on the level of the river; beaver ponds; and grassland. It offers a good opportunity for white-tailed deer and wild turkeys, wood ducks in spring, early summer, and early fall.

Viewing Information: Access to the site is on foot from two parking lots, one on the southwest corner of the site and the other accessible from the county road on the north boundary. Walking around in brushy areas can be heavy going, and the site can be wet. Hip boots can prove very useful, and in the spring and early summer may help you avoid wood ticks. Look for turkeys on the edges of the woody areas. Walk the sloughs to look for wood ducks. If you go to North River to view cranes, carry a flashlight. It will be dark when you leave the site.

Directions: *From U.S. Highway 30 at Hershey, go north 2.5 miles on the county road to the southwest parking lot (just across the bridge over the North Platte) or go 3 miles, turn right on the county road, and go approximately 1 mile to the north parking lot. The crane roost is southeast of the north parking lot.*

Ownership: NGPC (308) 535-8025

Size: 681 acres   **Closest town:** Hershey

The noses and ears of beavers are equipped with valves that close when the animal is under water. Beavers can even gnaw under water because they have lips that close behind their incisor teeth. ROCKY HOFFMANN

REGION 3: THE SANDHILLS

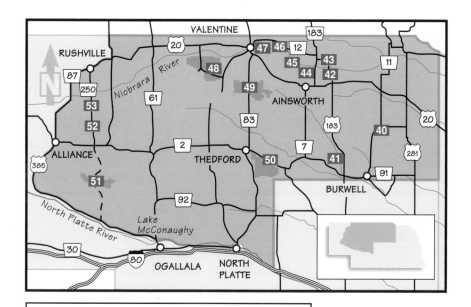

Wildlife Viewing Sites

40. Swan Lake Motor Route
41. Calamus Canoe Trail and Calamus Reservoir
State Recreation Area/Wildlife Management Area
42. Pine Glen Wildlife Management Area
43. Thomas Creek Wildlife Management Area
44. Keller Park State Recreation Area
and Keller School Land Wildlife Management Area
45. Niobrara Valley Preserve
46. Niobrara National Scenic River
47. Fort Niobrara National Wildlife Refuge
48. Samuel R. McKelvie National Forest/Merritt Reservoir
49. Valentine National Wildlife Refuge
50. Nebraska National Forest, Bessey Ranger District
51. Crescent Lake National Wildlife Refuge
52. County Road from Smith Lake
to Crescent Lake National Wildlife Refuge
53. Smith Lake Wildlife Management Area

The Sandhills

Ruddy duck. JON FARRAR

There are at least two features of Nebraska's Sandhills region that make it distinctive, if not unique. The first is the sand itself. With 19,300 square miles of dunes, it is one of the largest grass-stabilized dune fields anywhere. The second feature is water. The dunes sit atop a vast underground reservoir of water that is very close to the surface. In some of the valleys between dunes, the reservoir is exposed and there are wet meadows, marshes, lakes, and even constantly flowing streams. This underground reservoir was produced by the unique geology of the Sandhills—loose sand on the surface and thick deposits of more consolidated sands and gravels below. Early explorers wrote that the Sandhills was a desert that would never be of use to anyone.

The dunes are stabilized by grasses and forbs. The sand is not actively moving and drifting. Some of the plants are sand-adapted, growing only in sand or on sandy soils. Others are species that also grow in other places, like the tallgrass prairies to the east or the mixed-grass and short-grass prairies to the west. This particular association of plant species is so unusual that it is designated as a separate grassland type called "sandhills prairie." Although these plants are well adapted to soils and to the variations in rainfall common in the Great Plains, the Sandhills region is a fragile environment, extremely vulnerable to wind erosion if the thin, stabilizing layer of vegetation is broken.

Wetlands, lakes, and streams in the Sandhills are fed by groundwater rather than surface runoff. Lakes, both freshwater and alkaline, tend to be shallow and full of the plants and invertebrates favored by waterfowl, shorebirds, and wading birds. Alkaline wetlands have developed a unique association of plants, such as inland saltgrass, arrowgrass, and spearscale, that are adapted to or tolerant of alkaline soils. Like the stabilized dune field, Sandhills wetlands are a vulnerable environment, depending on high water tables. Disturbances such as ditching and pumping can have a significant effect on the water table and can affect wetlands far from the point of disturbance.

The Sandhills is perhaps the least disturbed of Nebraska's regions. Wildlife viewing sites in the Sandhills feature a relatively undiminished diversity of habitats and wildlife. But they are fragile. Even activities such as grazing can change the composition of vegetation in the Sandhills by encouraging the growth of plants adaptable to a certain grazing pattern.

The Sandhills illustrate an important principle of conservation: To be effective, conservation must be large scale, at a landscape level. Communities within the Sandhills—sandhills prairie or wetlands, for example—are interdependent. One cannot conserve wetland communities without conserving areas far from the wetlands and conserving the processes—here the hydrologic cycle—on which they depend.

Description: A scenic springtime drive along Nebraska Highway 11 past roadside wetlands and eastern sandhills grassland. At sunrise in April, prairie chickens and sharp-tailed grouse can be heard in their spring courtship displays. Several leks, or display grounds, are close enough to the road to be viewed with binoculars or a spotting scope. The wetlands are filled with Canada geese, mallards, pintails, shovelers, blue-winged and green-winged teal, herons, egrets, and sometimes pelicans. Swan Lake is also a good spot for redheads, canvasbacks, and ruddy ducks. Look for wild turkeys south of Swan Lake.

Viewing Information: This is mostly a driving tour, following Highway 11 south of the junction with Nebraska Highway 95. The area with the most wetlands is the dozen miles between the roadside picnic table and NE 95. There is little traffic along this road. Intersections between the highway and county roads make good places to pull off and listen for grouse and other birds. The road around the north side of Swan Lake has pulloffs and a boat ramp, which are good places to look over the lake. If you pull off along NE 11, get as far off the main part of the road as you can. But be aware—shoulders could be soft.

Directions: *From the junction of Nebraska highways 95 and 11, drive south on NE 11 toward Burwell.*

Size: 10- to 20-mile drive

Closest town: Burwell or Atkinson

Sharp-tailed grouse are less tolerant of agriculture than prairie chickens. Today their range in Nebraska is confined to the Sandhills where grass cover is still largely intact. ROCKY HOFFMANN

41. CALAMUS CANOE TRAIL AND CALAMUS RESERVOIR STATE RECREATION AREA / WILDLIFE MANAGEMENT AREA

Description: More than 50 miles of river through Nebraska's Sandhills, ending at Calamus Reservoir. Wildlife viewing opportunities are abundant, especially in spring. Species to watch for include ducks, herons, prairie chickens, beavers, muskrats, minks, river otters, white-tailed and mule deer, and soft-shelled turtles. Overhead you might see several species of hawks. On the reservoir there are large numbers of ducks and geese in fall, with some spending the winter. Bald eagles and golden eagles are present during waterfowl migrations. Bald eagles have nested on the upper end of the reservoir, and Canada geese nest on the upper reaches near the river. During fall and winter, prairie chickens and sharp-tailed grouse come into the Homestead Knolls campground to feed on dried berries.

Viewing Information: The scenic upper reaches of the river twist and turn along marshes and backwaters and offer excellent viewing of wildlife and marsh plants. Several access points along the canoe trail allow trips of various lengths. A map (available from NGPC) is essential. Learn the locations of the access points and campsites, because much of the land along the river is private. *PRIOR PERMISSION IS NECESSARY TO PUT IN, TAKE OUT, OR CAMP IN ALL BUT THE DESIGNATED SITES. THERE ARE MANY FENCES ACROSS THE RIVER. BE ALERT FOR FENCES ATTACHED TO BRIDGES.* Camping is allowed all along the shoreline of the reservoir, but cars must have a vehicle entry permit, available at the park headquarters.

Directions: *A county road goes west of U.S. Highway 183 along the Rock-Loup county line and crosses the Calamus River three times. THESE BRIDGES ARE THE ONLY PUBLIC ACCESS POINTS FOR THE RIVER. Other bridges require landowner permission to put in or take out. The headquarters for the reservoir is at Little York Point near the north end of the dam. From the west end of Burwell, follow the signs along the paved road to the reservoir.*

Ownership: River: private; Reservoir: USBR, leased to NGPC (308) 346-5666

Size: 50-mile canoe trail and 10,047-acre WMA and SRA

Closest town: Burwell

Nebraska has eight species of turtles. The largest is the snapping turtle, an aquatic hardshell turtle. The ornate box turtle is a common hardshell land turtle, most common in northern and central Nebraska. Another aquatic turtle is the smooth softshell turtle, which lives in Nebraska's rivers.

THE SANDHILLS

The Niobrara River Valley

The Niobrara River is a significant Great Plains river. It is the only east-west flowing Great Plains river without a major dam and reservoir. Sandbars on the river provide nesting habitat for rare and threatened species such as the least tern and piping plover, and the river is on the migration routes of bald eagles and whooping cranes. The river and its valley are scenic, and they provide recreation for an increasing number of people. For these reasons and more, parts of the central and lower Niobrara River have been designated part of the National Wild and Scenic River System.

A short, 30-mile stretch of the central Niobrara Valley, from Valentine east to Plum Creek, contains an exceptional mix of plant communities. This part of the river is often described as a "biological crossroads," where many plants and animals are at the limits of their natural ranges. Here, because of an unusual combination of geographical, geological, and hydrological conditions, five major plant communities converge. South of the river lies the Sandhills and the plant community called sandhills prairie; north of the river is the northern mixed-grass prairie typical of the Dakotas. Eastern deciduous forest—the bur oak, green ash, basswood, and black walnut forest typical of the eastern United States—survives here on the moist, wind-protected south bluffs of the river valley. Bluffs on the north side face into the sun. They are steep and dry with rocky soils, and they support pon-

Earless lizard. KEN BOUC

derosa pine woodlands more typical of the Black Hills and Rocky Mountains. Paper birch woodlands occupy the deep, cool, wet canyons of spring-fed streams on the south side of the Niobrara. These birch and other northern species have survived along the Niobrara since glacial times, when such species were common in Nebraska.

More than 200 bird species have been identified in this part of the river valley—eastern birds, western species, and some, like indigo and lazuli buntings, that have hybridized. The central Niobrara Valley, because it is one of the few places where the range of eastern deciduous forest overlaps the range of western coniferous forest, allows eastern and western species to mix. Elsewhere these groups are kept apart by the essentially treeless Great Plains.

Sites along the valley—the Niobrara National Scenic River (Site 46), Fort Niobrara National Wildlife Refuge (Site 47), and the Niobrara Valley Preserve (Site 45)—offer excellent opportunities to view this ecological crossroads.

42. PINE GLEN WILDLIFE MANAGEMENT AREA

Description: A scenic area along Long Pine Creek and Bone Creek, with native mixed-grass prairie descending into steep wooded canyons. The canyons are dominated by ponderosa pine, bur oak, and eastern red cedar. The area is popular for camping and hiking, and Long Pine Creek itself is a small trout stream with rainbow trout and an occasional brown trout. Pine Glen is a good area for both white-tailed and mule deer and wild turkeys year-round. During the spring migration it is a good site for viewing mixed-woodlands songbirds.

Viewing Information: There are parking areas on the east and west sides of Pine Glen WMA. The east parking lot has good access from the gravel county road; the west parking lot requires a drive along a two-track dirt road that is rutted and may be muddy. Use the east lot unless you have good clearance and four-wheel drive. Foot trails within the WMA are mowed.

Directions: From Bassett, take U.S. Highway 20 west to 1 mile east of Long Pine; turn north on the county road and go approximately 9 miles to the east parking lot. For the west parking lot: from the junction of U.S. highways 183 and 20 east of Ainsworth, turn north on US 183 and drive 7.5 miles to where US 183 bends west. Take the county road that continues straight for 0.5 mile; turn right (east) and go 2 miles to the parking lot.

Ownership: NGPC (402) 684-2921

Size: 960 acres   **Closest town:** Long Pine

White-tailed deer are named for their most distinctive feature—the large white tail that the animal raises like a flag as it bounds away. Whitetails were eliminated from Nebraska around the turn of the century but have made a remarkable recovery. They are most abundant in the woody cover of stream courses and shelterbelts in eastern Nebraska. BILL McCLURG

Description: High, open, mixed-grass prairie drops quickly into steep drainages of intermittent streams that feed Thomas and Lucky creeks. The canyons are heavily wooded with mature stands of ponderosa pine, eastern red cedar, and bur oak. In fall, the red sumac offers a brilliant fall display. The most reliable species to see at Thomas Creek WMA are white-tailed and mule deer and wild turkeys. During spring and fall migrations look and listen for black-and-white warblers and ovenbirds. Thomas Creek offers a limited opportunity to view sharp-tailed grouse and prairie chickens in the tree plantings in winter. Look for bobcat tracks in the sandy trails.

Viewing Information: Two parking lots offer access to Thomas Creek, one on the north side and the other on the west just off the county road. County roads are generally good but can be steep and muddy in wet weather. The north parking lot looks over the area. Hiking on Thomas Creek's unmarked trails can be strenuous, especially along the creeks and on steep, wooded canyons. Late winter and spring are good times to go because the trees are bare and visibility is better.

Directions: *From the junction of U.S. Highway 183 and Nebraska Highway 7, 2 miles south of Springview, go east on NE 7 for 2 miles. Turn south on the county road and go 2 miles to the northwest corner of Thomas Creek WMA. Go east here on the section-line road to the north parking lot access. For the west parking lot, instead of turning east, continue south for approximately 1.2 miles.*

Ownership: NGPC (402) 684-2921

Size: 1,154 acres   **Closest town:** Springview

The Niobrara River Valley divides Nebraska's sandhills prairie from the mixed-grass prairie more typical of the Dakotas. The Sandhills lies south of the river; to the north, soils are heavier and more clayey, and the prairie has none of the specialized sandhills plants.

THE SANDHILLS

44. KELLER PARK STATE RECREATION AREA AND KELLER SCHOOL LAND WILDLIFE MANAGEMENT AREA

Description: Two adjoining areas that together supply an interesting mix of habitats, including sandhills prairie, steep wooded canyons draining to Bone Creek, and open water in ponds in the recreation area. Keller Park is a reliable site year-round for white-tailed deer, an occasional mule deer, and hawks. During spring and fall waterfowl migrations, Keller Park is a stopover for puddle ducks such as teal, mallards, and shovelers. It is also a good spot for wild turkeys. Grassland birds to look for include grasshopper sparrows and dickcissels; woodland birds include American redstarts and scarlet tanagers.

Viewing Information: The northern part of the area is Keller Park. The land drains to Bone Creek and is steep and wooded mostly with ponderosa pine, bur oak, and red cedar. The WMA to the south is primarily upland prairie. Viewing is possible along park roads, but it is better to hike up the canyons formed by the intermittent streams that empty into Bone Creek. There are parking and facilities in the recreation area (permit required) and parking lots around the perimeter of the WMA (no fee).

Directions: *From the junction of U.S. highways 183 and 20 east of Ainsworth, go north 9 miles on US 183 to Keller Park SRA.*

Ownership: NGPC (402) 684-2921

Size: 840 acres   **Closest town:** Springview

Three species of teal migrate through Nebraska. The most abundant is the blue-winged teal. Look for them in April in small grassy-edged ponds and wetlands.
MIKE FORSBERG

Description: This premier viewing site is ecologically unique. The valley has been called the "biological crossroads of the Great Plains," and all of the prairie and woodland habitat types of the Niobrara Valley occur on the preserve. More than 200 species of birds have been identified here. It is a good site to view white-tailed deer and mule deer. The grassland on the preserve is maintained, in part, by a herd of 250 bison, roaming over 7,500 acres.

Viewing Information: Two self-guided nature trails, both of which feature short and long loops, lead you through the various habitats at the Niobrara Preserve. Brochures for the trails are available at the visitor center. The south river trail passes through paper birch stands, deciduous forest, tallgrass prairie, and marsh areas. The longer loop of this trail passes through sandhills prairie and includes a scenic view of the Niobrara River Valley. The short loop is 0.75 mile; the long loop is 1.75 miles. These two loops pass through pastures grazed by bison. *BISON CAN BE DANGEROUS. VIEW THEM FROM A DISTANCE.* The north trail is longer. The 1-mile short loop moves through river flood-plain, mixed-grass prairie, and pine forest. The longer loop (2 miles more) takes you to the canyon rim and follows it east. This trail has a few steep climbs. *THERE MAY BE RATTLESNAKES ON TRAILS.*

Directions: *From U.S. Highway 20 on the east side of Johnstown, go north 16 miles on the county road to the entrance to the Niobrara Valley Preserve.*

Ownership: The Nature Conservancy (402) 722-4440

Size: 55,000 acres   **Closest town:** Ainsworth

THE SANDHILLS

The Niobrara Preserve contains three forest types—eastern deciduous, ponderosa pine, and some paper birch trees of the northern boreal forest, the southern-most extension of that species on the Great Plains. KEN BOUC

Description: The portion of the Niobrara designated as a National Scenic River passes through many of the river's converging habitats—sandhills prairie on the south, mixed-grass prairie on the north, and three different forest types. The best wildlife viewing opportunities on the river are for turkey vultures, mule deer and white-tailed deer, coyotes, foxes, minks, muskrats, raccoons, wild turkeys, and, in the evening, several different species of bats.

Viewing Information: This is a popular canoeing river. The most popular stretch is the 30 miles between Fort Niobrara NWR and Rocky Ford (there is a fee for parking at Rocky Ford). Songbirds are best May 15 to June 15. May through September is best for wading birds and turkey vultures. Anytime is good for deer. Wildflowers are best May though July, with some late season flowers in August. October holds opportunities to see bald eagles. There are three public launch sites: Fort Niobrara NWR, Smith Falls State Park, and the Brewer Bridge. All other launch sites are privately owned. Many commercial outfitters offer canoe rentals and services; check with the Valentine Chamber of Commerce, 1-800-658-4024. *EIGHTY-FIVE PERCENT OF THE LAND THAT FRONTS THE RIVER IS PRIVATELY OWNED. PLEASE RESPECT THE LANDOWNERS' RIGHTS.*

Directions: *FORT NIOBRARA NATIONAL WILDLIFE REFUGE: from Valentine, go 4 miles east on Nebraska Highway 12. SMITH FALLS STATE PARK: from Valentine, go east on NE 12 for 15 miles, turn south, and go 4 miles to the park. BREWER BRIDGE: take NE 12 east to Sparks, then turn south and go 5 miles to Brewer Bridge.*

Ownership: Fort Niobrara NWR: USFWS (402) 376-3789; Smith Falls: NGPC (402) 376-1306; Brewer Bridge: Middle Niobrara Natural Resources District (402) 376-3241

Size: 76 miles   **Closest town:** Valentine, Ainsworth

Turkey vultures are scavengers rather than hunters. They do not have the sharp piercing talons of birds such as eagles or hawks. Vultures depend on highly developed senses of sight and smell to locate carrion. Look for them soaring along the Niobrara River or in the southeast at sites such as Indian Cave State Park. BOB GRIER

Description: As with other sites in the Niobrara River Valley corridor, Fort Niobrara NWR is a place where different ecosystems meet. The site offers excellent wildlife and habitat diversity, combining pine forest, eastern deciduous forest, boreal (northern) forest, sandhills prairie, and mixed-grass prairies. In addition to the many species of birds that can be viewed here, Fort Niobrara offers a year-round opportunity to see prairie dogs and enclosed herds of bison, elk, and white-tailed and mule deer. The refuge also maintains a herd of Texas longhorn cattle. Blinds are set up for viewing turkeys in the spring.

Viewing Information: A wildlife drive provides a good introduction to the diversity of plants and wildlife found on the refuge. Buffalo, elk, and deer can often be viewed as you drive through the prairie. In the prairie dog town you can watch these rodents and you may spot burrowing owls that nest in the town during the summer. The Fort Falls hiking trail is a good start to birding on the refuge. Go to the visitor center (open 8 A.M. to 4:30 P.M. Monday through Friday) for information explaining the history and ecology of the site, and for bird lists, trail maps, and brochures. The refuge is open during daylight hours.

Directions: *From Valentine, take Nebraska Highway 12 east 4 miles to the refuge.*

Ownership: USFWS (402) 376-3789

Size: 19,122 acres

Closest town: Valentine

THE SANDHILLS

Bison were a shaping force for the grasslands, encouraging the growth of grasses and plants that could tolerate trampling and grazing. JON FARRAR

48. SAMUEL R. MCKELVIE NATIONAL FOREST/ MERRITT RESERVOIR

Description: The major plant type found in this national forest is grass, not trees. These rolling sandhills grasslands are dry, and except for Merritt Reservoir in the southeast corner, offer no large body of open water to attract animals and birds other than those closely associated with the prairie. Look for grassland nesting birds like eastern and western kingbirds, lark sparrows, lark buntings, and meadowlarks. The Forest Service places a viewing blind near a sharp-tailed grouse dancing ground. It is available on a first-come, first-served basis in April. Merritt Reservoir attracts water birds, providing an opportunity to see pelicans, gulls, and great blue herons.

Viewing Information: A paved road runs through most of the McKelvie National Forest from north of the national forest to Merritt. You can walk out into the prairie or tree plantation at any point and find something interesting. In April, the Forest Service can provide a map to the four-person grouse blind. National forest lands have multiple uses that include hunting, horseback riding, and grazing. From May through October you may encounter gates used to control grazing. *LEAVE GATES THE WAY YOU FIND THEM.*

Directions: *To get to Merritt, take Nebraska Highway 97 south from Valentine approximately 22 miles to Merritt Reservoir. To approach the forest from the north, take U.S. Highway 20 west to the junction with Nebraska Highway S16F at Nenzel; turn south and go approximately 10 miles to the forest boundary.*

Ownership: McKelvie National Forest: USFS (308) 533-2257; Merritt Reservoir: USBR, leased to NGPC (402) 684-2921

Size: 115,700 acres   **Closest town:** Valentine

An oasis in the grass-mantled Sandhills, Merritt Reservoir offers water-oriented recreation and viewing opportunities for water birds in the spring. Eagles are here in March and April, and gulls and pelicans in April and May.
JON FARRAR

Description: In the heart of the dry, rolling dunes of the sandhills prairie, Valentine National Wildlife Refuge is an oasis, mixing lakes, marshes, and grasslands. Valentine Refuge is a migration stopover for as many as 150,000 ducks and a nesting site for blue-winged teal, mallards, pintails, gadwalls, and even diving ducks such as redheads and ruddy ducks. More than 260 species of birds (93 breeding species) have been sighted on the refuge, including herons, black terns, pelicans, and many songbirds. Long-billed curlews and upland sandpipers call from hill and fencepost. In spring, prairie chickens and sharp-tailed grouse gather for their elaborate courtship displays. Bald eagles and golden eagles are present in winter. White-tailed deer prefer the marshes and wooded lake margins; look for mule deer in the open hills. Other species include muskrats, coyotes, minks, raccoons, skunks, and weasels.

Viewing Information: There are viewing opportunities while driving roads within Valentine NWR and many more while walking. Wet weather or snow may limit driving. Information kiosks are located along the highway at both the north and south entrances. From U.S. Highway 83 north of the subheadquarters, you can park along the road near one of the refuge gates (pull completely off the highway) and take a short hike through the hills or along the wetlands. For a dramatic view of the Sandhills, drive to the refuge headquarters and take the next paved road south. Go about a half-mile and park at the start of the trail leading up to the old fire tower. The base of the tower (a half-hour hike) offers spectacular views of sandhills prairie, lakes, and marshes. In spring, observation blinds are set up to view the courtship displays of sharp-tailed grouse and prairie chickens.

Directions: *To the headquarters: take U.S. Highway 83 south of Valentine approximately 15 miles to Nebraska Spur 16B. Turn west on 16B and go 14 miles to the headquarters. The south entrance is 11 miles south of 16B on US 83.*

Ownership: USFWS (402) 376-3789

Size: 71,561 acres   **Closest town:** Valentine

THE SANDHILLS

Kangaroo rats inhabit the western two-thirds of Nebraska, especially the Sandhills. Kangaroo rats are unusual in that they can survive without drinking water. They can get all the water they need from food. They are difficult to view, but you can spot signs of them in areas of bare sand. Look for tracks with trailing undulating lines between them—the marks of the kangaroo rat's large hind feet and long tail.

50. NEBRASKA NATIONAL FOREST, BESSEY RANGER DISTRICT

Description: This unit of the Nebraska National Forest is named for Charles E. Bessey, whose crusade for tree planting in the Sandhills resulted in a 25,000-acre manmade pine and cedar "forest." After a fire in the 1960s, 20,000 acres still stand. But the dominant landscape in this 90,000-acre unit is rolling sandhills prairie with a little bit of the Dismal River along the south boundary and the Middle Loup River on the north. The wooded areas offer opportunities to see wild turkeys and woodland birds, including red-breasted and white-breasted nuthatches and clay-colored and chipping sparrows. The prairie offers opportunities to view sharp-tailed grouse and prairie chickens and other grassland birds such as common poorwills, lark buntings, and many others. It is a good site to view prairie dogs and nesting burrowing owls in summer, with some opportunity to see pronghorns, coyotes, and mule deer.

Viewing Information: Roads within the national forest are good for the most part, although in some places a high-clearance vehicle can be useful. For the locations of prairie dog towns and, in the spring, the locations of blinds for viewing grouse, contact the Forest Service. Hiking is permitted anywhere. Grazing from May to October is one of the many uses of the national forest. *PLEASE LEAVE GATES THE WAY YOU FIND THEM—OPEN OR CLOSED.*

Directions: *From Halsey, go west on Nebraska Highway 2 approximately 1.5 miles to the entrance.*

Ownership: USFS (308) 533-2257

Size: 90,448 acres   **Closest town:** Halsey

The dominant feature of the Bessey Division of the Nebraska National Forest is grass, not trees. Only 20,000 of the more than 90,000 acres have trees on them, and even those were hand planted. JON FARRAR

Description: Crescent Lake's hilly sandhills grassland and marsh-edged shallow lakes offer abundant food and cover for migrating and nesting shorebirds and water birds. The refuge is also a haven for grassland species such as sharp-tailed grouse, long-billed curlews, short-eared owls, white- and black-tailed jackrabbits, and small numbers of pronghorns. Principal shorebird species include avocets, willets, phalaropes, and sandpipers. Also look for bitterns, herons, cormorants, grebes, trumpeter swans, and pelicans. Trees attract migrating songbirds, among them kingbirds, bluebirds, and yellow-rumped warblers. Also look for coyotes, raccoons, badgers, great horned owls, and eagles.

Viewing Information: Crescent Lake is a four-season experience. Spring is best for migrating waterfowl and songbirds. Blinds are set up in April to view the courtship displays of sharp-tailed grouse. Summer is good for broods of goslings and ducklings, and, as waters recede to form mudflats, shorebirds. Winter presents opportunities for deer, pheasants, and golden eagles. The refuge has a self-guided auto tour—pick up a brochure at the refuge headquarters. *ROADS WITHIN THE REFUGE ARE NOT PAVED, BUT ARE PASSABLE BY MOST VEHICLES. SOME TRAILS ARE FOUR-WHEEL DRIVE ONLY. THE ROADS TO THE REFUGE ARE BAD—SOMETIMES PAVED, SOMETIMES GRAVELED, AND SOMETIMES SINGLE-LANE COUNTRY ROADS.* The headquarters is not staffed at all times.

Directions: *From Oshkosh, take the county road north 28 miles to the refuge headquarters. Or, from Nebraska Highway 2 just east of Lakeside, go south on the county road 28 miles to the headquarters.*

Ownership: USFWS (308) 762-4893 (refuge), (308) 635-7851 (office)

Size: 45,849   **Closest town:** Oshkosh

THE SANDHILLS

Double-crested cormorants are common migrants in Nebraska. They breed on sparsely vegetated islands like those on Crescent Lake National Wildlife Refuge, on the margins of reservoirs, or in the skeletons of flooded trees. JACK CURRAN

Description: A scenic drive through open sandhills prairie, passing by Sandhills lakes and wetlands. Many of these lakes and wetlands are alkaline—basins with no outlets and poor subsurface drainage, which prevents salts from escaping. These wetlands are full of invertebrate life, providing food for nesting shorebirds such as American avocets, willets, and Wilson's phalaropes, and for large numbers of migrating shorebirds and waterfowl.

Viewing Information: This road offers good opportunities for roadside viewing of shorebirds and waterfowl, but it is little traveled and in poor condition. It's driveable, but you have to take it easy. During spring and fall migrations the area can be full of many species of ducks. Mid-April through mid-June are best for shorebirds and water birds such as cormorants.

Directions: *From Rushville, go south on Nebraska Highway 250 approximately 30 miles to Smith Lake. Continue on the county road another 60 miles to Crescent Lake NWR. Note: there are no facilities south of Rushville until you reach Lakeside, and then not until Oshkosh, another 60 miles.*

Ownership: Private

Size: 150 miles from Rushville to Oshkosh

Closest towns: Rushville, Lakeside

American bitterns, though large, are often difficult to see. Their color disguises them well, as does their habit of freezing in place, bill up, doing their best to look like a cattail or bulrush stalk.
BOB GRIER

53. SMITH LAKE WILDLIFE MANAGEMENT AREA

Description: A typical Sandhills lake—that is, a lake largely supplied by groundwater in a fold of the surrounding Sandhills. The level of Smith Lake is maintained by controlling the water flowing in and out along Pine Creek. There are cottonwoods along the shoreline, and cedars and ponderosa pines have been planted thickly on the north and west. During the spring migration, Smith Lake draws good numbers of ducks, first divers such as redheads and canvasbacks, then teal, mallards, pintails, and other dabblers. It is a good spot to view pelicans, herons, egrets, and grebes. The trees attract migrating songbirds such as northern orioles and yellow-rumped warblers. The grasslands attract grassland-nesting species like grasshopper sparrows.

Viewing Information: Spring is the best time to go to Smith Lake WMA for wildlife viewing. Waterfowl begin to arrive after the ice is off the lake in late February and usually stay around until April. The songbird migration peaks in May. Roads to the site are good, and there are parking lots around the perimeter of the WMA.

Directions: *From Rushville, take Nebraska Highway 250 south 23 miles to Smith Lake WMA.*

Ownership: NGPC (308) 762-5605

Size: 640 acres (222-acre lake)

Closest town: Rushville

Canvasbacks are diving ducks. Their feet are set far back on their bodies, making it easier for them to dive to feed but also making it difficult to walk. The best viewing of diving ducks in Nebraska is on Sandhills lakes such as Smith Lake.
JON FARRAR

REGION 4: THE PANHANDLE

Nebraska's Panhandle rises to 5,400 feet, almost a mile higher than the state's lowest point along the Missouri. As elevation increases east to west across Nebraska, rainfall decreases. The Panhandle is the driest part of Nebraska, and grasses here grow shorter. The region once fed deer, elk, pronghorns, and vast numbers of bison. In Nebraska today the Panhandle is the only area to support elk and even a few transplanted bighorn sheep.

But there is more to it. There is considerable habitat and wildlife diversity within the Panhandle, from Lake McConaughy and the North Platte River in the south, through shortgrass plains, to extensions of the Rocky Mountain pine forest in the Wildcat Hills and the Pine Ridge (and Nebraska's only designated wilderness, Soldier Creek), and finally to the Oglala National Grassland. Sites in the Panhandle offer the chance to view ducks and geese as well as pronghorns and mule deer; eagles as well as prairie grouse; prairie dogs, wild turkeys, and even, rarely, river otters.

Coyotes are among the most adaptable of wildlife species, surviving changes in habitat and extravagant efforts to exterminate them. JON FARRAR

Wildlife Viewing Sites

54. Lake Ogallala
55. Clear Creek Wildlife Management Area
56. Wildcat Hills State Recreation Area and Nature Center/
    Buffalo Creek Wildlife Management Area
57. Scotts Bluff National Monument
58. North Platte National Wildlife Refuge, Winters Creek Lake Unit
59. Kiowa Wildlife Management Area
60. Agate Fossil Beds National Monument
61. Gilbert-Baker Wildlife Management Area
62. Fort Robinson State Park/Peterson Wildlife Management Area
63. Soldier Creek Wilderness
64. Nebraska National Forest, Pine Ridge Unit
65. Chadron State Park
66. Ponderosa Wildlife Management Area
67. Oglala National Grassland
68. Metcalf Wildlife Management Area

54. LAKE OGALLALA

Description: Lake Ogallala provides one of the best winter opportunities to view bald eagles in Nebraska. As many as 374 eagles have been seen here at a time; viewers often see more than 100. Water enters Lake Ogallala from Lake McConaughy through the Kingsley Hydroplant. Turbulence created by the action of the turbine maintains open water all winter and forces fish to the surface. The number of eagles here depends on winter weather. During mild winters, when other areas are not frozen over completely, eagles are more dispersed.

Viewing Information: Eagles can be viewed as they scan the open water from cottonwoods on the south shore or from the ice near areas of open water below the hydroplant. The best eagle viewing is from the north side of Lake Ogallala near the plant. Lake Ogallala also attracts waterfowl in the late fall and winter, with some birds staying the winter. It is a good site for winter birding, and occasionally you can spot coyotes and foxes. A permit is required at the state recreation area.

Directions: *From Ogallala, go north on Nebraska Highway 61; head east where U.S. Highway 26 and NE 61 split; follow NE 61 to Kingsley Dam. The road to the north shore of the lake is just before the dam. To go the state recreation area, go over the dam and turn right.*

Ownership: The Central Nebraska Public Power and Irrigation District, leased to NGPC (308) 535-8025

Size: 339 acres, plus 320-acre lake   **Closest town:** Ogallala

Redheads are often confused with canvasbacks. Both species are diving ducks and are often seen together. Female redheads will even lay their eggs in the nests of canvasbacks. JON FARRAR

Description: At the upper end of Lake McConaughy, Clear Creek WMA has cottonwood groves in the flat floodplain of the river, willow-covered islands, wet meadows, seasonal wetlands, grasslands, and cropland. Bluffs on the south side offer an elevated view of the river. The habitat diversity in the area creates good viewing of migrational concentrations of teal, pintails, and mallards; diving ducks at the upper end of the area; geese; and long-billed curlews, yellow-legs, sandpipers, and Wilson's phalaropes. Less common water birds include sandhill cranes, pelicans, trumpeter swans, cinnamon teal, and western grebes. There are large populations of white-tailed deer here and good opportunities to view wintering bald eagles. Clear Creek WMA is among the best areas in the state to see river otters.

Viewing Information: The largest concentrations of waterfowl and shorebirds are in March and April. Viewing is possible from many areas, but perhaps the best is from the duck blinds in the controlled hunting area south of the check station. Check with the NGPC office in North Platte to make sure that the blinds are open. Most of Clear Creek WMA is managed as a refuge during the fall. Roads in the refuge area are closed November through February. These roads offer good opportunities to view pheasants and deer at other times. Pelicans winter at the site and usually concentrate here in late May; best viewing is at the upper end. Streams in the upper end offer occasional opportunities to view great blue herons and egrets. Sandhill cranes are here during March and April. *ROADS ALONG THE SOUTH SIDE OF THE AREA REQUIRE HIGH CLEARANCE AND, WHEN MUDDY, FOUR-WHEEL DRIVE.*

Directions: *From Lewellen, go east on Nebraska Highway 92 for 5 miles; turn south (right) and go 1 mile to the check station.*

Ownership: NGPC (308) 535-8025

Size: 6,000 acres

Closest town: Lewellen

THE PANHANDLE

There are two species of skunks in Nebraska—the familiar striped skunk and the less common and less well-known spotted skunk. The spotted skunk, first recorded in Nebraska in 1893, is probably not a Nebraska native, but it spread quickly into every county in the state. However, these skunks have been far less adaptable to habitat changes than their striped cousins. Populations of spotted skunks have declined quickly, and today they are rare.

56. WILDCAT HILLS STATE RECREATION AREA AND NATURE CENTER/BUFFALO CREEK WILDLIFE MANAGEMENT AREA

Description: Areas of open mixed-grass prairie along with timbered ridges and canyons. High bluffs overlook the North Platte River Valley. Ridges and canyons are covered in ponderosa pine, cedar, and shrubs such as mountain mahogany and skunkbush sumac. Featured species are raptors, including golden eagles, prairie falcons, merlins, red-tailed hawks, Swainson's hawks, and ferruginous hawks. It is also a good site for mule deer and white-tailed deer and for coyotes in winter. Both eastern and western bluebirds are here in early spring. Nuthatches, grosbeaks, juncos, and other songbirds can be viewed at the nature center's feeders in winter. During summer look for violet-green swallows and common poorwills. Broad-tailed hummingbirds have been seen here. The southern part of the SRA is an enclosed preserve with display herds of bison and elk.

Viewing Information: A good place to start is at the new nature center, where you can see displays of area wildlife, get maps and brochures, learn about the ecology of the area, and walk several nature trails. Buffalo Creek is a more primitive experience; access is on foot or horseback only, trails are not marked, and there are no designated campsites or facilities. A pond in the middle of the WMA offers some opportunity for waterfowl viewing. Fees are required for the nature center and the recreation area, but not for Buffalo Creek WMA.

Directions: *WILDCAT HILLS NATURE CENTER: From Scottsbluff, go south on Nebraska Highway 71 for 12 miles to the site. BUFFALO CREEK WMA: From Melbeta (east of Gering) on NE 92, turn south on the county road and go 1 mile. Turn west and go 1 mile; turn south again and go 3 miles; turn west again and go 1.5 miles; turn south and go 1 mile to Buffalo Creek WMA.*

Ownership: NGPC (308) 436-3777 (SRA) or (308)-762-5605 (WMA)

Size: 935-acre SRA; 2,880-acre WMA

Closest town: Gering (SRA); Melbeta (WMA)

The American burying beetle—a large orange-and-black beetle—depends on carrion for survival. Records show that these beetles once inhabited 35 states but survive now in only four—Nebraska, Rhode Island, Oklahoma, and Arkansas. They are an endangered species on both federal and state lists.

Description: A landmark for westward-minded pioneers, Scotts Bluff, a largely siltstone and sandstone escarpment rising out of the surrounding mixed-grass prairie, reveals a cross-section of geologic history going back 34 million years. Wildlife include white-throated swifts and cliff swallows nesting in stunted trees or cliff sides during summer and magpies and kestrels year-round. Prairie falcons nest here; they can be seen flying near cliff-face nests during summer. The largest percentage of grassland wildlife—like the grass itself—lives mostly underground. Rabbits, mice, and pocket gophers all burrow out of sight of the foxes, badgers, coyotes, and snakes that still inhabit the area. The only poisonous snake is the prairie rattler. The monument's hiking trails are a great place to view prairie wildflowers in spring and summer.

Viewing Information: Though the emphasis is on history, the monument offers opportunities to view wildlife by car or along a 1.6-mile hiking trail. Guide booklets for the trail are available at the visitor center. *THE ROCK ALONG THE SUMMIT TRAIL IS SOFT AND CRUMBLY—STAY ON THE PAVEMENT. THERE ARE RATTLESNAKES IN THE AREA—THEY ARE SHY BUT WILL STRIKE IF THREATENED.*

Directions: *From Gering, go west on Nebraska Highway 92 for 3 miles to the entrance road.*

Ownership: NPS (308) 436-4340

Size: 3,000 acres   **Closest town:** Gering

THE PANHANDLE

Badgers can be found throughout Nebraska. They tend to be most common in grasslands and near woodland edges. They are largely nocturnal. JON FARRAR

58. NORTH PLATTE NATIONAL WILDLIFE REFUGE, WINTERS CREEK LAKE UNIT

Description: Winters Creek Lake is a natural wetland that has been enhanced to store irrigation water. Unlike many such lakes, the water level stays fairly constant, allowing shoreline vegetation to grow and making this lake the best place on the refuge for wildlife viewing. Shoreline vegetation such as cattails and bulrush attracts western and pied-billed grebes and black and Forster's terns. The upland areas provide good springtime birding.

Viewing Information: The best roadside viewing is along the south side of the area. There are two parking lots along this road; the lot at the end of the road has a boat ramp. Internal combustion engines are prohibited on the lake. Winters Creek Lake is a good place to view wildlife from a canoe or on foot. The site is closed October 1 through January 15 to provide sanctuary for migrating waterfowl.

Directions: *From the town of Minatare, take Stonegate Road north 7 miles to Lake Minatare. Follow the road west and north around Lake Minatare, passing the road into the state recreation area (stop at the headquarters for information and a brochure), cross the canal, and turn left at the junction. There are kiosks at the entrance to Winters Creek.*

Ownership: USFWS (308) 635-7851

Size: 500 acres   **Closest town:** Minatare

Three species of grebes commonly nest in Nebraska. Western grebes are easily viewed because they court and nest in areas with open water. JON FARRAR

59. KIOWA WILDLIFE MANAGEMENT AREA

Description: Kiowa WMA is one of the North Platte River Valley's few remaining alkaline wetlands. These wetlands, along with freshwater marshes and seeps, make wildlife viewing at Kiowa a year-round experience. Alkaline wetlands (low-lying areas where high water tables, poor drainage, and high evaporation combine to concentrate salts) are favored by American bitterns, herons, egrets, ibises, pied-billed grebes, eared grebes, and pelicans. The marshes and seeps attract 2,000 to 3,000 snow geese in spring, and Canada geese, blue-winged teal, cinnamon teal, and mallards nest here. The seeps maintain some open water all year, and wintering populations of mallards have been estimated at 25,000 to 30,000.

Viewing Information: The north half of Kiowa WMA is mostly wetland and open water. The south half is upland managed largely for pheasants and deer with shelterbelts and cropland. On the east side of the site, along the paved road from Morrill, is a parking lot with an observation deck that overlooks the freshwater marshes and open water. Gravel roads allow you to drive the perimeter of the site. The northwest end of the area gives a fairly good overlook of the alkaline wetlands. Winter and spring are the best seasons for ducks and geese. Spring is best for migrating shorebirds like Baird's and white-rumped sandpipers, snipe, yellowlegs, avocets, willets, and phalaropes.

Directions: *From U.S. Highway 26 at Morrill, turn south on the road at the west edge of town and go approximately 3 miles to the east parking lot.*

Ownership: NGPC (308) 762-5605

Size: 546 acres   **Closest town:** Morrill

Alkaline and freshwater wetlands at Kiowa WMA provide habitat for about 70 species of birds, including shorebirds such as lesser yellowlegs. Shorebird migration begins in March and peaks in late April to early May. JON FARRAR

THE PANHANDLE

Description: Famous for wildlife long since extinct, the monument lies in an area of shortgrass and mixed-grass prairie in the Niobrara River Valley. This prairie is largely undisturbed and has good plant diversity. The site offers good opportunities for viewing white-tailed deer and fair opportunities for mule deer. Backwaters and oxbows in the river create marshes and meadows that provide an opportunity for muskrats and some wading birds, but the site is better for grassland nesters—lark buntings or upland sandpipers, for example, or Say's Phoebe on the mixed-grass prairie or on rocky bluffs. Swainson's hawks are summer residents and ferruginous hawks nest nearby. A trail leads from the interpretive center to fossil beds partway up the bluffs.

Viewing Information: The monument has good access, a new interpretive center, and offers wildlife viewing from roads and trails. Deer are best viewed from the roads at dusk year-round; late spring and summer are best for songbirds. Soaring hawks can be viewed overhead. Visitors occasionally see coyotes. *WATCH FOR RATTLESNAKES.*

Directions: *From the junction of U.S. Highway 26 and Nebraska Highway 29 at Mitchell, go north on NE 29 for 34 miles. Turn east on the River Road and go 2.5 miles to the interpretive center.*

Ownership: NPS (308) 668-2211

Size: 2,300 acres   **Closest town** Harrison

Ferruginous hawks are buteos, or soaring hawks. They are often seen overhead in open country like that found in Nebraska's Panhandle. Ferruginous hawks nest in tree crotches and on the ledges of rocky outcrops.
BOB GRIER

Description: Along the Pine Ridge escarpment (see page 86), Gilbert-Baker contains four large canyons that drain to Monroe Creek. The canyons are rugged and steep, and forests are dominated by ponderosa pine. Along Monroe Creek are stands of green ash, cottonwood, and two species found in Nebraska only in the northern part of this county—western birch and mountain maple. Gilbert-Baker is one of the few places in Nebraska to see least chipmunks; look on the shrubby slopes leading up from the creek bottoms. The rough canyons with open areas in the trees are good places to view deer. Look for Cooper's hawks, kestrels, western tanagers, and common flickers in the creek bottoms, and common poorwills and pinyon jays along the forested ridgetops. There are opportunities to view coyotes and even elk, which move in and out of the area. Overhead you may see turkey vultures, golden eagles, and prairie falcons.

Viewing Information: Access is on foot from three parking areas; two are near the north boundary near the camping area and trout pond, and the other is on the south end. Hiking is fairly rugged. Best viewing is in spring and summer for birds; year-round for deer; and spring, summer, and fall for wild turkeys.

Directions: *From U.S. Highway 20 at Harrison, go north on the paved road 5.5 miles to the campground parking lot.*

Ownership: NGPC (308) 762-5605

Size: 2,537 acres   **Closest town:** Harrison

Elk were once common in Nebraska, but today they can be viewed only in Pine Ridge sites like the Nebraska National Forest, Fort Robinson, and Gilbert-Baker WMA. BOB GRIER

THE PANHANDLE

The Pine Ridge

The Pine Ridge escarpment is a range of sandstone hills about a hundred miles long that forms an arch across the northwestern corner of Nebraska's Panhandle. The ridge is named for the ponderosa pines that cover its slopes. Today's landscape was carved by erosion, giving it a harsh, rugged beauty. As in other parts of Nebraska, the geographic range limits of many species of plants and wildlife overlap here, giving sites in the Pine Ridge a high diversity of plant and animal life.

The topography of the Pine Ridge, with abrupt changes in slope and twisting canyons and ravines, makes for abrupt changes in habitat as well. North-facing slopes are cooler and retain more moisture, allowing denser growth of pines. Southern and western slopes dry quickly, favoring more drought-tolerant plants and mixed grasses. In the cool, moist bottoms of the draws and ravines, deciduous trees like cottonwood, green ash, hackberry, and aspen can survive. Wildlife communities are equally mixed, with habitats suitable for both white-tailed deer and mule deer, sharp-tailed grouse and wild turkeys, and both eastern and western varieties of birds.

As with other environments, diversity within the plant and wildlife communities of the Pine Ridge is vulnerable to changes brought about by human action. Ponderosa pine dominates our attention in the Pine Ridge. Ponderosa pine is drought tolerant and is well

Bighorn sheep. BOB GRIER

BOB GRIER PHOTO

adapted to withstand drying winds. But in times past, the Pine Ridge may have had fewer pines, with trees in scattered areas and in canyons. There once was more prairie. The change has been brought about largely because of fire control.

Prairie and pine forest represent different successional stages of plant communities. Following a disturbance—fire, for example—forbs and grasses are the first to show lush regrowth. Pine seedlings among the grasses grow slowly, only gradually dominating the area. Without disturbances, the forest will finally become a dense stand of pine trees, which are the "climax" species of this community. Plant succession in the Pine Ridge is more complex because of the different

Prairie rattlesnake. JON FARRAR

moisture and temperature conditions presented by its topography of steep slopes, rocky buttes, deep canyons, and creek bottoms. In some areas, because of exposure to the sun and wind, the climax vegetation remains the mixed grasses of the prairie. In cool, moist canyons, the climax species are deciduous trees like cottonwood, willow, aspen, and boxelder.

62. FORT ROBINSON STATE PARK/PETERSON WILDLIFE MANAGEMENT AREA

Description: Fort Robinson State Park and Peterson Wildlife Management Area are typical of the Pine Ridge, with mixed-grass prairie, rocky outcroppings, and pine-covered buttes. They have been much changed by fire, and the ponderosa pine forest has been replaced by vigorous growths of native grasses and shrubs. Fort Robinson has become a better site for viewing bighorn sheep. Lewis's woodpeckers are now being seen in the burned areas, making use of the dead timber. This is also a good place to see prairie dogs, wild turkeys, golden eagles, prairie falcons, barn owls, and western songbirds like mountain bluebirds, western tanagers, common poorwills, and white-throated swifts. Peterson WMA is more primitive than Fort Robinson—neither camping nor trails are developed.

Viewing Information: Opportunities to see bighorns in Nebraska are rare, but it is often possible to see them on rocky buttes north of the fort complex at Fort Robinson. Hiking and horseback trails from Highway 20 east of the fort complex and Soldier Creek Road sometimes offer views. The Smiley Canyon Scenic Drive passes through an enclosure with exhibition herds of bison and then down through Smiley Canyon at the north end of the Peterson Wildlife Management Area. Mountain biking is allowed on some of the trails within the park. Primitive camping is permitted within the WMA. There are no fees at Peterson WMA.

Directions: From Crawford, drive 2 miles east on U.S. Highway 20 to the fort complex. Follow Smiley Canyon Drive to Peterson WMA.

Ownership: NGPC (308) 665-2900 (Ft. Robinson), (308) 762-5605 (Peterson WMA)

Size: Fort Robinson: 22,000 acres; Peterson WMA: 2,640 acres

Closest town: Crawford

Raccoons are among the most adaptable of wildlife species, able to take advantage of nearly any situation. For example, raccoons will make a home or bed in coyote dens, badger burrows, old beaver lodges, or even a crow or hawk nest. Look for raccoon tracks—the front feet look like small hands—in muddy areas along wooded streams and lakes.

63. SOLDIER CREEK WILDERNESS

Description: Another area extensively burned in the 1989 fire, Soldier Creek Wilderness is being allowed to recover naturally. It is said that the more open, grass-covered landscape here today resembles photographs taken a hundred years ago, when fires were uncontrolled.

Viewing Information: There is a well-developed trail system through much of Soldier Creek Wilderness. The trailhead is located at the end of the Soldier Creek Road through Fort Robinson State Park. No vehicles or bikes are allowed on the trails, but you are welcome to bring your horse. Corrals are available at the trailhead. Water is reliable for horses from springs and from Soldier Creek, but you should pack in enough water for your own use. The most active seasons for wildlife viewing are spring, summer, and fall. Birders should visit during all of these seasons. The area is good for many Pine Ridge species—white-tailed and mule deer, wild turkeys, hawks, eagles, coyotes, and foxes (bobcats occur here too, but they are even more elusive than coyotes and foxes).

Directions: Access to the Soldier Creek Wilderness is through Fort Robinson State Park. From the fort complex at the park, turn onto Soldier Creek Road and go approximately 7 miles to the trailhead and parking area.

Ownership: USFS (308) 432-4475

Size: 9,600 acres   **Closest town:** Crawford

The western tanager is one of a number of birds that summer in the Pine Ridge, but nowhere else in Nebraska. BOB GRIER

THE PANHANDLE

Fire and Rain

Fort Robinson State Park and Peterson Wildlife Management Area (Site 62), and the Soldier Creek Wilderness (Site 63) form a complex of sites. As you drive or hike through these areas you will be looking at the aftereffects and recovery of two significant natural events—a 1989 fire that burned some 48,000 acres of ponderosa pine forest, and the torrential rains and floods of 1991.

The forest fire was unusually damaging to the pines here. It is estimated that 90 percent of the large ponderosa pines were destroyed. It had been a long time since this forest had burned, so the fire had abundant ground fuel to work with and a succession of young trees to climb its way into the crown of the older ponderosas. Without this "fuel ladder," the older trees would have survived and the forest would look very different than it does today.

In the park and in the Soldier Creek Wilderness you see two different management plans at work. In the park, trees have been planted to take the place of those that were burned. Because of its "wilderness" designation, Soldier Creek is being allowed to recover at its own pace of succession and regrowth. It is estimated that, given the rate that ponderosa pines grow and scatter their seeds, a return to "day of the fire" condi-

DON CUNNINGHAM PHOTO

tions might take 300 to 500 years. But no one wants it to regain the condition that allowed the 1989 fire to be so destructive. Relatively frequent fire has advantages.

The fire and the subsequent flooding have been very beneficial to the forest in the bottoms of the draws. The fire cleared dead trees and old trees that had become decadent; trees such as boxelder have resprouted from the roots and stumps of the old ones and are now flourishing. The bottoms that were scoured clean or silted in by flood waters proved fertile ground for cottonwood seedlings, and new groves of cottonwood are doing well.

All this has had its effect on wildlife. Areas that once were covered in dense growths of pine now grow brushy plants like chokecherry and wild plum interspersed with grassy areas and annual plants. This new growth is vigorous, nutritious, and evidently palatable to many different kinds of wildlife, particularly deer, wild turkeys, and perhaps even elk. The buttes northwest of the old sheep enclosure (see Site 62) have seen increased use by bighorn sheep. Densely treed areas of once-prime white-tailed deer habitat are now more open and are seeing increased use by mule deer.

DON CUNNINGHAM

BOB GRIER

Description: This unit of the Nebraska National Forest joins Chadron State Park and Ponderosa WMA (Sites 65 and 66) to form a complex that typifies the habitats and viewing opportunities in the Pine Ridge. This mix of short-grass and mixed-grass prairies, barren rock outcrops, and wooded canyons suits the needs of animals unusual to Nebraska—bighorn sheep, elk, least chipmunks, fringed-tailed bats, and others. Plants such as silky orophaca and Hood's phlox have adapted to the harshness of the barren rock outcrops. Typically, these "rock plants" grow low to the ground in compact clumps. Their tiny, narrow leaves or even needles are adaptations to conserve moisture and to avoid the harsh wind.

Viewing Information: The Pine Ridge Unit is scattered over a wide area. Roads within the forest vary from well-maintained gravel to four-wheel drive only. Stop at the Pine Ridge Ranger District Office (open 7:30 A.M. to 4:30 P.M. Monday through Friday) to pick up a map and check road conditions. The national forest is managed with multiple uses in mind; you may encounter hunters in season or cattle grazing May through October. *LEAVE GATES THE WAY YOU FIND THEM.*

Directions: *From Chadron, go 3 miles south on U.S. Highway 385 to the ranger district office.*

Ownership: USFS (308) 432-4475

Size: 52,000 acres   **Closest town:** Chadron

"Rock plants" such as alpine bladderpod and Hood's phlox grow in dry, rocky, and exposed locations. Look for them at Scotts Bluff National Monument, Agate Fossil Beds National Monument, Gilbert/Baker Wildlife Management Area, and the Pine Ridge Division of the Nebraska National Forest. JON FARRAR

65. CHADRON STATE PARK

Description: Nebraska's oldest state park, Chadron is typical of this part of the Pine Ridge with its grassy pine stands, heavily forested steep slopes, rocky bluffs, and brushy creek bottoms. The park is surrounded by the Pine Ridge Unit of the Nebraska National Forest and offers facilities that serve as a good base camp for an exploration of the forest. Deer and wild turkeys are prominent, especially in the creek bottoms and more heavily forested areas. Red crossbills, with beaks adapted to extracting seeds from pine cones, pinyon jays, western tanagers, and western bluebirds are typical of the area.

Viewing Information: There are marked hiking, mountain biking, and cross-country ski trails throughout Chadron State Park, taking you through most of the different habitats in the park and in the Pine Ridge region.

Directions: From just west of Chadron, take U.S. Highway 385 south 8 miles to Chadron State Park.

Ownership: NGPC (308) 432-6167

Size: 974 acres   **Closest town:** Chadron

66. PONDEROSA WILDLIFE MANAGEMENT AREA

Description: Located at the southwest edge of the complex of sites that includes the Nebraska National Forest and Chadron State Park, Ponderosa WMA has many of the same scenic qualities and habitat diversity as other Pine Ridge sites. It is one of the best sites in Nebraska for viewing white-tailed deer and mule deer. Bird species include mountain bluebirds, wild turkeys, prairie falcons near the buttes, and hairy and downy woodpeckers. Squaw Creek crosses the area along its southern border, offering views of fox squirrels, cottontail rabbits, and an occasional great blue heron.

Viewing Information: Access to Ponderosa WMA is excellent; a county road follows Squaw Creek and mowed service roads make good hiking trails. There are parking lots throughout the area. The "Rim of the World" trail (foot access from parking lot 5) offers a long-range overview of the area. Deer and wild turkeys can be viewed year-round. Look for bluebirds, prairie falcons, woodpeckers, and porcupines in spring, summer, and fall. A resident manager can provide additional information.

Directions: From Crawford, go 3 miles south on Nebraska highways 2 and 71, turn east, and go 4 miles on the county road to the site. The county road continues through the site and along the creek.

Ownership: NGPC (308) 762-5605

Size: 3,660 acres   **Closest town:** Crawford

THE PANHANDLE

Description: A large area characterized mostly by native mixed-grass prairie, with wooded streambeds and "badlands"—steep, eroded, sparsely vegetated formations created by water and wind erosion on layers of siltstone, sandstone, and clay. Toadstool Park is such an area, named for narrow clay pedestals topped with slabs of sandstone that looked like huge toadstools (most of the large ones have fallen). The Oglala Grassland is the best place in Nebraska to view pronghorns and a popular place to view prairie dog colonies along the site's northern border. Overhead you are likely to see red-tailed hawks, Swainson's hawks, ferruginous hawks, and golden eagles. Swift foxes can be found here too, but they are rare and not very active during the day. These opportunist foxes take advantage of vehicle-killed animals, so they are occasionally seen along roadsides. Oglala is also a good site for coyotes and badgers.

Viewing Information: Roads in the Oglala Grassland vary from paved state highways to four-wheel drive only. Most of the roads are gravel and are passable except after a rain or a snowstorm. Stop at the district office south of Chadron to pick up a map of the grassland, get directions to the prairie dog towns, and learn about any hazards or interesting opportunities. The office is open 7:30 A.M. to 4:30 P.M. Monday through Friday. Grassland birds such as upland sandpipers, chestnut-collard longspurs, lark buntings, or Brewer's blackbirds are seen year-round, but the most active times for birds are late spring and summer. There is a small campground at Toadstool Park, with tables, restrooms, and water. It makes a good starting place to explore the site.

Directions: *TO TOADSTOOL PARK: go 4 miles north from Crawford on Nebraska highways 2 and 71, turn northwest on Toadstool Road, and go 15 miles. TO THE PINE RIDGE RANGER DISTRICT OFFICE: go 3 miles south of Chadron on U.S. Highway 385.*

Ownership: USFS (308) 432-4475

Size: 94,000 acres   **Closest town:** Crawford

Pronghorns are often called antelope, but they are not related to true antelope. They are unique animals in that they have hollow horns, like cattle, but shed them every year, like deer shed their antlers. As a result, many biologists classify them as a separate family in which they are the only genus and species.

68. METCALF WILDLIFE MANAGEMENT AREA

Description: The most remote of the Pine Ridge sites, Metcalf WMA has heavily timbered canyons interspersed with mixed-grass prairies, but it does not have the exposed buttes typical of other sites. Metcalf WMA is noted for its diverse pine-woodland vegetation and features many of the same species as other Pine Ridge sites. There are better opportunities here to see elk, which move in and out of the area.

Viewing Information: Metcalf WMA is relatively isolated; there is no vehicular traffic within the area and little other traffic nearby. Hiking trails lead into the middle of the area from both the south and east sides, where there are parking lots.

Directions: *From the west edge of Hay Springs, go north on the county road 4 miles; turn east and go 1 mile; turn north again and go 6 more miles to the south edge of Metcalf WMA.*

Ownership: NGPC (308) 762-5605

Size: 3,068 acres

Closest town: Hay Springs

Mountain bluebirds are a western species, most commonly seen in Pine Ridge sites such as Metcalf WMA. During the migration look for them in flocks in open country, perching on roadside fences or telephone wires; during the nesting season look to the edges of open pine stands and burned areas.
JON FARRAR

THE PANHANDLE

WILDLIFE INDEX

This index features some of the most sought-after wildlife species in Nebraska and the best sites to see them. The numbers refer to the site number, not the page number.